MW00559187

Celine Rousseau

La Table by Celine

Exquisite food art that
brings nature to the plate

PRESTEL

MUNICH – LONDON – NEW YORK

Cherry

Food and nature hold the keys to a certain nostalgia for me. They possess the power to conjure up warm emotions and stir treasured memories from within.

Having grown up and spent time living in diverse parts of the world, my memories are a rich tapestry woven from different cultures, all intertwined with tender moments around nature and food. There are the days of sun-kissed cherry picking in California, the picnics with ethereal cherry blossom confetti in Tokyo, seashell collecting on the beaches of Normandy, and family camping trips with s'mores amid the golden autumn leaves in Korea.

This book and the recipes it contains draw inspiration from these carefree, happy moments I've spent in nature. Each chapter flows through the seasons, reflecting what I associate with each. From the buzzing bees and blossoms of spring to the diverse palette of summer fruits, darting fish, and shells of summer, to the falling leaves and mushrooms of autumn, each recipe tells a story of nature through my eyes.

My wish is that this book, as it encapsulates these stories, will transport you to your own joyous, marshmallow-soft and sweet memories, so you can recreate those moments around your own table.

Most of the recipes you'll find here evoke specific reminiscences of mine. From apple pie to *melon pan* (bread) and kimchi fried rice, these are the dishes I grew up with and now cook with my family and friends. After all, the best recipe, I believe, is one that you and your loved ones enjoy. If you already have a favorite recipe—your grandmother's divine chocolate tart or your father's signature pizza dough—I encourage you to stay true to it. My greatest joy would be to know that these recipes inspired you to add a touch of art or visual flair to your own nostalgic flavors, or perhaps helped you create new, wonderful memories to be cherished in the years to come.

I hope that by the end of this journey, you'll have your very own table, imbued with your personal touches and memories. La Table by [Your Name]: make it uniquely yours.

Cherry Blossom

Cherry blossoms, with their delicate and ethereal beauty, symbolize a new beginning and the fleeting nature of life. In Japan, both the school and fiscal year start in April, when the blossoms are in full bloom. My first day of school, my first day at a job, the start of a new project: many new chapters in my life were celebrated with the natural confetti of pink and white cherry blossom petals.

Hanami, literally composed of *hana* (花) and *mi* (見), is a Japanese word for "flower viewing" but more specifically "cherry blossom viewing." It's the highlight of springtime in Japan, when everyone gathers outside to enjoy the gossamer blossoms that last only for about two weeks. Witnessing them bloom and fall in such a short period of time evokes a sense of *monono aware*: bittersweet awareness, the joy and pathos of feeling transience, passing, and impermanence.

This poignant awareness reminds everyone
to cherish and savor each passing moment,
embracing the evanescent nature of all things.

This chapter is inspired by my springtime
in Japan, cherry blossom trees, and *hanami*.
Whether you're planning a *hanami* picnic
under the boughs or simply enjoying the season
from the comfort of your home, these cherry
blossom-inspired creations will bring the magic
of this tradition, and the remarkable beauty of
impermanence, to your table.

Hanami Chirashi Bento

As cherry blossoms burst into bloom across Japan, people flock to popular picnic spots to celebrate the arrival of spring. Essential to this festive occasion is the array of beautiful, colorful *hanami bentos* (lunch boxes). Prepared by home cooks, local restaurants, or renowned chefs, these special bentos are packed with pink-hued delicacies and elaborately curated cherry blossom-themed dishes that capture the season in their ingredients and presentation.

This recipe is a spring take on chirashi sushi, inspired by the *hanami bentos* I saw in Japan. Chirashi sushi, a style of sushi served on joyous occasions and at parties, requires no shaping or molding of the rice. The dish consists of sushi rice simply decked with various colorful toppings. My version is made with my go-to sushi ingredients: salmon, avocado, eggs, and salmon roe, scattered atop lightly seasoned sushi rice with pink pickled radish to add a hint of spring.

RECIPE ON THE NEXT PAGE

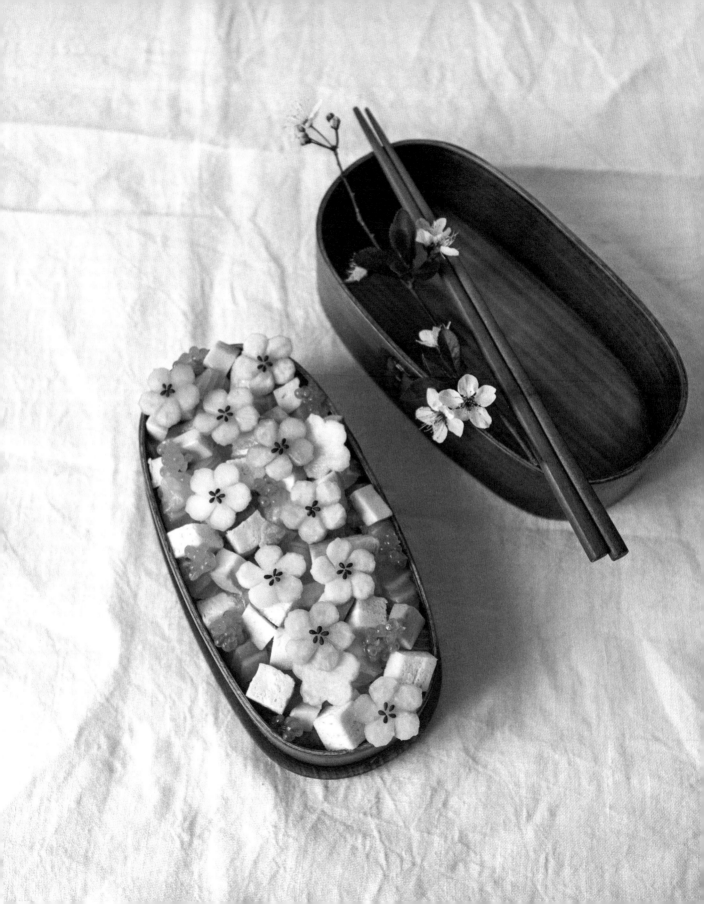

FOR THE RADISH PICKLE
⅓ daikon radish
1 teaspoon yukari powder
    (shiso rice seasoning)
2 tablespoons sugar
4 tablespoons rice vinegar
4 tablespoons water
1 teaspoon salt
Black sesame seeds (optional)

FOR THE OMELET
3 eggs
½ tablespoon tsuyu
½ tablespoon water
Oil

FOR THE SUSHI RICE
350 g (1¾ cups) freshly cooked
    sushi rice
1 tablespoon rice vinegar
½ tablespoon sugar
¼ teaspoon salt

FOR THE TOPPING
½ avocado, cut into cubes
50 g (4 tablespoons) salmon roe
180 g (6 ounces) sushi-grade
    salmon, cut into cubes

TOOLS
Cherry blossom-shaped cookie
    cutter, 3 cm (1 in) diameter
Tamagoyaki pan (Japanese
    omelet pan)
Empty mesh tea bag (used for
    bagging one's own tea)

To make the pickled radish, slice the radish to 4 mm (⅛ in) thickness and cut into cherry blossom shapes using a cookie cutter, adding more petal details with a knife if needed (optional).

In a small saucepan, combine the sugar, rice wine vinegar, salt, and water. Bring the mixture to a boil over medium heat and stir until the sugar has dissolved. Remove the saucepan from the heat. Add the yukari powder, placed in an empty mesh tea bag.

Transfer the cherry blossom-shaped radish to a glass jar or container and pour the vinegar mixture over the top, making sure the radish is fully covered. Cover the jar or container and place it in the refrigerator for at least 2 hours, or overnight for a darker pink color.

To make the sushi rice, combine the rice vinegar, sugar and salt in a small bowl and stir until the sugar is dissolved. Transfer the cooked sushi rice to a large bowl and pour the vinegar mixture over the rice. Using a rice paddle or spoon, gently fold the vinegar mixture into the warm rice until well combined, and let it cool to room temperature.

To make the omelet, combine the eggs, tsuyu and water in a bowl, whisking until thoroughly mixed. Place a tamagoyaki pan over medium-low heat and use a paper towel to apply a thin layer of cooking oil to the surface.

Pour a small amount of the egg mixture into the pan, ensuring it spreads evenly by tilting the pan. When the bottom of the egg has set but the top is still slightly runny, use two spatulas to roll the egg toward you, creating a small roll.

Push the roll to the far end of the pan and pour another thin layer of the egg mixture so it covers the remaining surface of the pan (and slides under the roll). When the new layer has set but the top is still slightly runny, repeat the gesture of rolling the existing egg roll toward you. It will pick up more layers as it rolls.

Repeat the process until you have used up all of the egg mixture. When the omelet is fully cooked, remove it from the pan and let it cool for a few minutes. Cut the omelet into small cubes.

Assembly: Fill a bento box or bowl with sushi rice, spreading it evenly to cover the bottom of the box/bowl. Arrange the toppings on the sushi rice. Add a few slices of pickled radish on top and decorate with black sesame seeds for the cherry blossom details.

Sakura Soba Noodles

Soba noodles adorned with flowers in shades of pink—naturally
tinted with beetroot juice—is a dish reminiscent of cherry blossom
petals cascading down on a breezy spring day.

— SERVES 2 —

FOR THE BASE NOODLE
125 g (1 cup) buckwheat flour
125 g (1 cup) all-purpose flour
125 ml (½ cup) water

FOR THE DARK PINK FLOWERS
50 g (⅓ cup) buckwheat flour
50 g (⅓ cup) all-purpose flour
50 ml (scant ¼ cup) beetroot juice

FOR THE LIGHT PINK FLOWERS
50 g (⅓ cup) buckwheat flour
50 g (⅓ cup) all-purpose flour
25 ml (scant ⅛ cup) beetroot juice
25 ml (scant ⅛ cup) water

TOOLS
Flower-shaped cookie cutters
   (5 mm and 1 cm/⅛ in and ⅓ in)
Chopsticks

*Note: My preference is for soba made
using the nihachi ratio (meaning a
2:8 ratio of 20% wheat flour to 80%
buckwheat flour). But for this sakura
soba, I used 50% buckwheat flour
and 50% wheat flour. Without gluten,
buckwheat flour has limited elasticity,
making the dough extremely fragile.
Thus, the more wheat flour you add,
the easier it is to work with the dough.*

To make the base noodle, sift the
buckwheat and wheat flours into
a large bowl, then slowly add the
water and mix until the dough comes
together. Knead well until the dough
has a smooth surface and feels like
your earlobe.

Sprinkle a bit of flour on a flat surface
and roll out the dough using a rolling
pin to about 1.5 mm (¹⁄₁₆ in) thickness.

Sprinkle the dough with flour and
fold it over gently so the longer sides
meet. Repeat another 2–3 times, fold-
ing the same way, lengthwise (rather
than creating a square), and dusting
with more flour each time you fold to
prevent sticking. Cut the soba into
5–7 mm (⅕–⅓ in) strips using a sharp
knife.

To make the dark and light pink
flowers, sift the buckwheat and wheat
flours into a large bowl, then slowly
add the beetroot juice or beetroot
juice and water and mix well until the
dough comes together. Knead well
until the dough has a smooth surface
and feels like your earlobe.

Sprinkle a bit of flour on a flat surface
and roll out the dough using a rolling
pin to about 1.5 mm (¹⁄₁₆ in) thickness.
Cut out into flower shapes using
flower-shaped cookie cutters.

To assemble, apply a bit of water to
the pink flowers and press them with
chopsticks so they stick to the base
noodle.

Bring a large pot of water to boil and
cook the noodles for about 2 minutes
until tender. Rinse with cold water
and chill in a bowl of ice water.

You can serve the noodles cold (with
Japanese mentsuyu, grated daikon
radish, nori, and green onions) or
hot (in a broth with green onions and
other toppings).

Cherry Blossom Rice Chips with Branch Sticks

Fragile and delicate cherry blossom rice chips served with branch-shaped breadsticks feel like spring served in a bowl. I recommend accompanying them with charcuterie, cheese, and olives for a spring *aperitivo*.

MAKES 20 CHIPS AND ABOUT 15 BRANCHES

FOR THE BRANCHES
85 ml (⅓ cup) lukewarm water
½ teaspoon sugar
½ teaspoon instant yeast
150 g (1¼ cups) all-purpose flour
½ teaspoon salt
20 g (1½ tablespoons) olive oil

FOR THE CHERRY BLOSSOM RICE CHIPS
8–10 sheets rice paper
50 g (½ cup) cooked short grain rice
1 tablespoon red beetroot, juiced
Oil for frying

TOOL
Kitchen thermometer

To make the branches, combine the water, sugar, and yeast in a small bowl. Let the mixture sit for about 5–10 minutes, or until it bubbles up and becomes frothy.

In a large bowl, combine the flour and salt. Pour the yeast mixture into the dry ingredients, mixing until a dough forms. Gradually incorporate the olive oil while kneading. Continue kneading for about 10 minutes until the dough is smooth and elastic.

Place the dough in a bowl, cover it with plastic wrap or a clean kitchen towel, and let it rise in a warm place for about an hour, or until it doubles in size.

Preheat the oven to 190°C (375°F).

Once the dough has risen, divide it into 15–16 small pieces. Roll each piece into a long, thin stick about 25 cm (10 in) in length and 2–3 mm (⅒ in) in diameter. To mimic the look of tree branches, attach smaller branches to some of the sticks as needed.

Arrange the branches on a baking sheet. Bake for about 10 minutes, or until crispy and golden brown.

To make the cherry blossom rice chips, carefully cut the rice paper into about 20 five-petaled shapes (5 cm/2 in diameter for the petals) and 20 smaller five-petaled shapes (2 cm/¾ in diameter for the interior pollen layer) using kitchen scissors.

To color the interior pollen layer, brush on the beetroot juice and let it dry fully. Add a bit of beetroot juice to the bowl of cooked rice to dye it pink.

To assemble the flowers, using a bit of cooked rice as "glue," place the pink pollen paper on the petal paper and press it down. Top it with a dab more of pink rice. You should end up with two rice paper layers, glued together with rice and topped with a dab more.

Fully dry the flowers by air drying or dehydrating them in the oven. (I like to dry them in a 70°C (160°F) oven for about 30 minutes, though you can also shorten this step if pressed for time).

Heat oil in the pan until it reaches 180°C (350°F). Fry the assembled flowers in the oil for a few seconds until puffed up. Remove them from the pan with kitchen tongs and place on paper towels to cool.

Season the rice chips with salt or your favorite seasoning and serve with the branches.

Cherry Blossom Meringue Branches

Light, airy, and sweet cherry blossom-shaped meringues
on tree branch-shaped breadsticks are as ephemeral
as cherry blossoms' fleeting delight. Savor each morsel,
one blossom at a time.

FOR THE BRANCHES
85 ml (⅓ cup) lukewarm water
½ teaspoon instant yeast
½ teaspoon sugar
150 g (1¼ cups) all-purpose flour
½ teaspoon salt
20 g (1½ tablespoons) unsalted
   butter, room temperature

FOR THE MERINGUE BLOSSOMS
4 egg whites
½ teaspoon cream of tartar
A pinch of salt
200 g (1 cup) granulated sugar
1 teaspoon vanilla extract

OPTIONAL
Pink food coloring
Sprinkles

TOOLS
Piping bag with a cherry
   blossom nozzle

To make the branches, in a small bowl, combine the water, yeast, and sugar. Let the mixture sit for about 5–10 minutes or until it bubbles up and becomes frothy.

In a separate large bowl, combine the flour and salt. Add the yeast mixture to the dry ingredients. Mix until a dough forms.

Gradually add the softened butter, kneading as you go. Continue to knead for about 10 minutes until the dough becomes smooth and elastic.

Place the dough in a bowl, cover with plastic wrap or a clean kitchen towel, and allow to rise in a warm place for about an hour, or until doubled in size.

Preheat the oven to 190°C (375°F).

Once the dough has risen, divide it into 15–16 small pieces. Roll each piece into a long, thin stick about 25 cm (10 in) in length and 2–3 mm (⅒ in) in diameter. To mimic the look of tree branches, attach smaller branches to some of the sticks as needed.

Place the shaped dough on a baking sheet with parchment paper and bake for about 10 minutes, or until crispy and golden.

To make the meringue blossoms, preheat the oven to 100°C (210°F).

Separate the egg whites from the yolks, ensuring no yolk gets into the whites. Whip the egg whites and cream of tartar with a pinch of salt until frothy using a stand or hand mixer.

Gradually add the sugar, one spoonful at a time, while continuing to whip the egg whites. Once the mixture forms stiff, glossy peaks, add the vanilla extract. To test the meringue, rub a small amount between your fingers— it should feel smooth, not grainy. If it's grainy, whip a bit longer.

For pink cherry blossoms, add a bit of pink food coloring (optional).

Transfer the meringue to a piping bag fitted with a cherry blossom nozzle. Arrange the branches on the baking sheet with some space in between them. Pipe meringue on top of the branches to resemble cherry blossoms. Add sprinkles in the middle for petal details, if desired. Around the branches, pipe additional individual meringues so they look like flowers that fell from the branches.

Bake the meringues for about 1 hour or until they peel off the parchment paper easily. Turn off the oven and let the meringues and branches cool completely inside (about 1–2 hours).

Serve the flowering branches in a bowl or vase. Arrange the meringue flowers around them.

Kkot (꽃) Rice Cakes

In Korea, a tradition similar to Japan's *hanami* is called *kkot-nori* (꽃놀이), meaning "flower play." This custom, dating to the Three Kingdoms era, involves heading out into nature during springtime for picnics in the countryside, in mountains, in fields, or by the water. On such occasions, people admire and gather flowers, creating various rice cakes such as *hwajeon* (화전; flower rice cake), which are made with glutinous rice flour and decorated with edible flowers. Other variations can be naturally colored with flower, berry, or plant powders and may even include a sweet filling.

While the practice of making rice cakes al fresco is not as prevalent today, Koreans continue to enjoy *kkot-nori* through leisurely strolls, simple picnics, or by creating flower-inspired rice cakes at home. These cherry blossom-shaped treats are a way to indulge in the beauty of spring in a classic Korean "art of living" way.

RECIPE ON THE NEXT PAGE

100 g (⅔ cup) short grain rice flour

25 g (generous ⅛ cup) mochiko
(sweet rice flour)

125 ml (½ cup) hot water

A pinch of salt

Food coloring (pink, yellow) or
natural coloring powders (berries
or flowers): ½ teaspoon each or
more for darker colors

TO SERVE
Sesame oil or neutral oil
Simple syrup or honey

TOOL
Bamboo (or metal) steamer basket

Note: Traditionally, natural ingredients
are used to color the rice cake: omija
(Korean five berries) powder for pink,
chija (gardenia fruit) or sweet pumpkin
powder for yellow. These powders also
add their own subtle flavors. If you can
find these ingredients or want to replace them with other natural powders
that can lend both color and flavor,
I encourage you to give it a try.

In a large mixing bowl, combine the rice and mochiko flours with a pinch of salt.

Gradually add the hot water to the flour mixture, stirring constantly with a wooden spoon or spatula until a smooth dough forms. Knead the dough with your hands for 2–3 minutes until it becomes elastic and pliable.

Divide the dough into 4 portions: 3 around 80 g (2.82 ounces) each and 1 around 10 g (0.35 ounce). Add a bit of food coloring to each of the three larger portions to create white, light pink, and slightly darker pink dough. To the remaining smaller portion, add yellow food coloring. Keep the dough covered.

To shape the flower petals, take a small amount of dough from one of the larger portions (about half a teaspoon), roll it into a ball, and then pinch one end into a point. Repeat to create 5 petals.

To form the flower, place the 5 petals together, pinched ends facing inward.

To finish, take a small amount of the yellow dough, roll it into a tiny ball, and place it at the center of the flower. Use a toothpick to add lines as petal details.

Repeat this process for the rest of the dough, creating white, light pink, and dark pink flowers. Keep them covered with plastic wrap or a damp cloth until ready to steam.

Line a bamboo steamer basket with a piece of damp cheesecloth or parchment paper. Arrange the rice cakes in the steamer basket, making sure they're evenly spaced and don't touch each other. Place the basket over a pot of boiling water, ensuring the water level is below the bottom of the steamer. Cover the steamer with a lid and steam the rice cakes for about 15–20 minutes.

Carefully remove the steamer basket from the pot and let the rice cakes cool slightly. Brush the surface of each rice cake with sesame oil or neutral oil. Serve with simple syrup or honey.

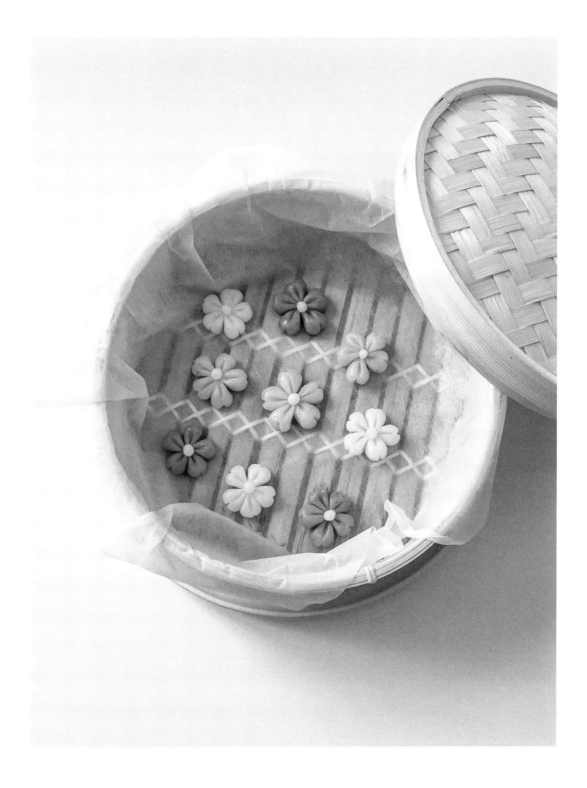

Asparagus with Whipped Feta Cherry Blossoms

Whipped feta piped on asparagus in the shape of cherry blossoms and topped with lemon zest and mint leaves makes a light and refreshing starter or side, capturing both the flavor and the look of spring.

———————————————— SERVES 2 ————————————————

100 g asparagus (10–12 slim stems), tough ends trimmed
100 g (3½ ounces) feta
75 g (⅓ cup) Greek yogurt
1 tablespoon olive oil
½ garlic clove, minced
1 tablespoon lemon zest
Mint leaves and shelled, cooked green peas to garnish

TOOL
Piping bag with a cherry blossom nozzle

Bring a large pot of salted water to a boil. Add the asparagus and cook for about 3 minutes, until just tender (less or more depending on the thickness of the asparagus). Drain the asparagus and immediately transfer to a bowl of ice water. Once cooled, drain and pat the asparagus dry using paper towels. Arrange the asparagus on a plate.

In a blender, blend the feta, Greek yogurt, olive oil, and garlic until smooth.

Transfer the mixture into a piping bag with a cherry blossom nozzle. Pipe the whipped feta onto the asparagus, add lemon zest to the center of each piped "blossom," and garnish with mint leaves and shelled green peas before serving.

Daisy

Daisies are wildflowers that grow in many places in the world—small, unassuming and common. But these yellow-and-white beauties have captivated the hearts of poets, artists, lovers and children with their humble charm. Perhaps it's because they're accessible. They spring up almost everywhere, from mountain meadows and fields to city sidewalks and parks. This makes them an easy flower to play with: most of us have fond memories of making daisy chains or playing the classic game of "loves me, loves me not," plucking off petals one by one to discover if our crush loves us or not.

Ordinary though they seem, daisies' real magic lies in their capacity to bring out happiness in tender moments. They make the ordinary seem extraordinary.

"Daisy"
Margherita Pizza

This is a reimagined Margherita pizza, with mozzarella as the white petals and yellow cherry tomatoes as the flowers' golden center. I wanted to highlight the elegant simplicity of both the iconic dish and the daisy itself, as well as the way they both summon a sense of uncomplicated, demure happiness.

MAKES 1 PIZZA (24 CM/9 IN)

Use a store-bought pizza dough or refer to the dough recipe below.

FOR THE DOUGH
¼ teaspoon dry yeast
¼ teaspoon sugar
80 ml (⅓ cup) lukewarm water
(mix two parts of cold water
and one part hot water)
125 g (1 cup) flour, Tipo 00
or pizza flour
¼ teaspoon salt

TOPPINGS
50–75 g (¼–½ cup) tomato sauce
6–7 mini mozzarella balls
3–4 yellow cherry tomatoes
5–6 basil leaves

Note: If you choose to use store-bought dough, take it out of the fridge 15 minutes before preparation. Unpack the dough and unroll it.

In a small bowl, combine the yeast, sugar, and lukewarm water. Mix well and let the mixture stand for 5–10 minutes until bubbles form.

In a large bowl, combine the flour and salt. Pour the yeast mixture into the dry ingredients and stir until well combined.

When the mixture becomes difficult to stir, transfer the dough onto a lightly floured surface and knead for approximately 10 minutes. Cover it with a cloth or bowl and let it rise at room temperature for an hour. (You can let it rest overnight in the fridge; take it out 1–2 hours before use and bring it to room temperature.)

Once the dough has risen, preheat the oven to 220°C (425°F). Line a baking sheet with parchment paper. Lightly flour a surface, flatten the dough, and stretch it into a round shape (with hands or a rolling pin). Spread the tomato sauce over the dough and bake it for about 10 minutes. Remove it from the oven.

Meanwhile, slice the mini mozzarella balls to a thickness of 3 mm (⅛ in) and halve the yellow cherry tomatoes. Arrange 5–7 mozzarella slices on the partially baked pizza to form flower petals, placing a halved cherry tomato at the center.

Return the pizza to the oven and bake for another 5 minutes or until the crust is golden brown.

Garnish with fresh basil leaves before serving.

Lemon Tart with Daisy Meringues

Here is a spring twist on lemon meringue tart. Its refreshing citrus flavor will awaken your taste buds, while the daisy flowers against a yellow background will brighten your table. Serve yourself a slice of spring!

MAKES 1 TART (18 CM/7 IN)

FOR THE TART SHELL
200 g (around 13) digestive biscuits
    (wholemeal biscuits)
100 g (7 tablespoons) butter, melted

FOR THE LEMON CURD
2 eggs plus 2 egg yolks (reserve
    the whites for the meringue)
100 g (½ cup) sugar
1 tablespoon cornstarch
A pinch of salt
Zest of 1 lemon
100 ml (½ cup) lemon juice
80 g (5½ tablespoons) butter,
    cold and cubed

FOR THE MERINGUE
2 egg whites
100 g (½ cup) sugar
A pinch of salt

OPTIONAL
Mint leaves

TOOLS
Tart tin (18 cm/7 in) with
    a removable bottom
2 piping bags with a round tip
Kitchen thermometer

To make the tart shell, in a food processor, pulse the digestive biscuits until they are finely crushed. Add the melted butter and pulse until well combined. Press the crumb mixture into the base and sides of the tart tin. Refrigerate the tart shell to set.

To make the lemon curd, whisk together the eggs, sugar, cornstarch, and salt in a medium-sized mixing bowl.

In a medium-sized non-reactive saucepan, heat the lemon zest and juice until simmering, then pour them slowly into the egg mixture, whisking constantly to avoid curdling the egg.

Transfer the mixture back into the saucepan and cook over medium heat, stirring continuously, until thickened so that a finger run over the back of the spoon leaves a mark. Strain the mixture through a sieve to remove the zest and any scrambled pieces. Add butter to the strained mixture and blend well using a blender or whisk.

Reserving 1 tablespoon of the lemon curd, pour the rest into the tart shell, smoothing the surface with a spatula. Chill in the fridge for at least 3 hours or until set.

To make the meringue, combine the egg whites, sugar, and salt in a glass or metal bowl. Place the bowl over a pot of boiling water, ensuring that it does not touch the water. Whisk the mixture until it reaches 70°C (160°F) and the sugar has completely dissolved. When you rub a bit of the mixture between your fingers, it should feel smooth, not gritty.

Remove the bowl from the pot of water. Using an electric whisk, beat the mixture until very stiff peaks form.

Fit a piping bag with a small round tip. Fill the piping bag with the meringue, then pipe the meringue into daisy petal shapes on top of the lemon curd filling. Fill another piping bag with the reserved lemon curd and pipe it at the center of the daisy petals. Garnish with mint leaves and serve.

Croissants with Mascarpone Cream and Lemon-Curd Daisies

Flaky, buttery croissants almost need no embellishment.
But these daisy flowers made of vanilla mascarpone cream
and tangy lemon curd offer an effortless way to elevate a basic
breakfast into an indulgence.

Savor these at home accompanied by a cup of coffee as morning
sunlight streams through the windows, or enjoy them al fresco
in the garden for a breakfast picnic!

SERVES 6

6 fresh croissants

150 g (⅔ cup) mascarpone
150 ml (⅔ cup) heavy cream
30 g (¼ cup) powdered sugar
1 teaspoon vanilla extract

A half batch of the lemon curd
from the Lemon Tart with Daisy
Meringues recipe (p. 33)

TOOLS
2 piping bags

In a medium bowl, beat the mascarpone until smooth.

In a separate bowl, combine the heavy cream, powdered sugar, and vanilla extract, and whip until stiff peaks form.

Fold the whipped cream into the mascarpone and gently mix until well combined.

Transfer the mixture to a piping bag fitted with a round nozzle or cut the end with a kitchen scissor. Similarly, transfer the lemon curd to a second piping bag and make a tiny cut in the end.

Pipe the cream onto the croissants to create daisy patterns. Then pipe the lemon curd to create each daisy's yellow center.

Agedashi "Daisy" Tofu with Grated Radish and Ginger

Agedashi tofu is a Japanese appetizer that makes a warm welcome to any dining experience. With its crispy exterior and silky, smooth interior, this lightly fried tofu—paired with a warm dashi broth with a hint of ginger—provides a lovely texture and flavor. Just as fresh daisies help you herald the approaching spring and subsequent seasons, this simple dish will be a gentle invitation into the meal to come.

MAKES 3–4 SERVINGS

FOR THE TOFU
1 package of semi-firm or firm tofu (net weight 300–350 g/ 10½–12⅓ ounces)
¼ daikon radish, micro-grated
2–3 cm (1 in) piece of fresh ginger, micro-grated
4 tablespoons potato starch
1 green onion, thinly sliced

FOR THE TSUYU SAUCE
300 ml (1¼ cups) water
2 tablespoons soy sauce
2 tablespoons mirin
1 teaspoon dashi powder

Oil for frying

TOOLS
6 cm (2½ in) flower-shaped cookie cutter
Kitchen thermometer

Drain the tofu and slice into approximately 2 cm (¾ in) thick slices. Use a cookie cutter to cut each slice into a flower shape. Remove excess water by patting dry with a paper towel, then letting the tofu sit between paper towels for 10–15 minutes.

Meanwhile, grate the daikon, squeeze out excess water, and set aside. Grate the ginger and set aside.

To make the tsuyu sauce, bring the water to a boil in a small or medium saucepan. Add the soy sauce, mirin, and dashi powder. Turn off the heat and set aside.

Heat a wok or skillet of frying oil to 160–170°C (320–340°F). Pat the tofu dry again with paper towels. Using a plate or bowl, coat the tofu with the potato starch, dusting off any excess. Making sure pieces do not touch each other, fry the tofu in the hot oil for a few minutes, until its surface is crispy and golden brown.

Place the tofu in a serving bowl and arrange the grated radish and ginger on top in little mounds to resemble a daisy. Serve with warm tsuyu sauce and thinly sliced green onion.

Fried Egg Daisies on Kimchi Fried Rice

In Korea, daisies are sometimes called "fried egg flowers" due to the duo's resemblance. White petals encircling a vivid yellow center indeed bring to mind a flawlessly fried sunny side-up egg.

Kimchi fried rice is a quintessential Korean comfort food, traditionally prepared with leftover rice. It is a simple and accessible dish that can be made by anyone. Despite its ubiquity, every household believes they make the best version, with their own homemade kimchi, secret ingredients, or unique steps to personalize the dish. Ultimately, it represents the taste of nostalgia and home.

Often, a fried egg completes the dish. In much the same way that modest daisies add a touch of charm to a green meadow, the fried sunny side-up egg acts as a pleasant finishing touch to kimchi fried rice. To commemorate this connection, I've topped kimchi fried rice with daisy-shaped fried eggs.

―――― SERVES 1 ――――

1 tablespoon neutral oil
50 g (about ½–1) leek or green onion, thinly sliced
50 g (¼ cup) diced ham
100 g (½ cup) of kimchi, chopped
200 g (¾ cup) cooked rice, cooled down (leftover rice is best)
½ tablespoon mirin
½ tablespoon soy sauce
½ tablespoon sesame oil
1 chicken egg or 3–4 quail eggs

OPTIONAL
1 sliced green onion
Roasted seaweed (gim) strips

TOOLS
Flower-shaped cookie cutter
    (10 cm/4 in for a chicken egg;
    6 cm/2½ in for a quail egg)
Cooking spray

Note: You can modify the recipe according to your kimchi's characteristics, as it is the key ingredient that will determine the dish's flavor. If your kimchi is not sour or fermented enough, add a splash of vinegar; if it's too sour, balance it with some sugar. Adjust the amount of soy sauce depending on its saltiness.

To make the kimchi fried rice, heat the neutral oil in a pan or wok over medium-high heat. Add the leek or green onion and stir-fry until fragrant. Add the diced ham and continue frying for about 2 minutes. Stir in the kimchi and continue frying for another 2 minutes. Add the rice and break it up with a wooden spoon, mixing everything until well combined. Add the mirin. Add the soy sauce, if needed, to taste. Mix everything well and drizzle with the sesame oil at the end.

To make the daisy-shaped fried eggs, apply neutral oil to the cookie cutter using a brush or cooking spray.

Heat a frying pan over low heat. Add a little oil to the pan and place the cookie cutter in the center. Crack an egg into the cookie cutter. To position the yolk in the center, you can separate the egg white and yolk ahead of time, adding the egg white first and then placing the yolk in the center of the cookie cutter. Cook the egg as desired.

Remove the fried egg from the pan and let it cool for 1 minute. Using a knife or teaspoon, cut around the inner edges of the cookie cutter and gently press down on the egg white to separate the egg from the cookie cutter.

Serve the fried rice topped with daisy-shaped eggs, sliced green onions, and roasted seaweed (gim) strips.

Tulip

With their radiant colors and long stems
that exude elegance, tulips appear in early
spring, grabbing everyone's attention and
announcing the season's debut. Tulips
instantly add brilliance to a space, whether
an interior or a garden or park. The moment
you bring a vase of these minimalist blooms
into a room, it's like the transition from
black-and-white to color film, as though
you had opened the blinds to let in radiant
sunlight. The world seems richer, warmer,
more joyful. That is the power of tulips.

Crêpes Sucrées with Strawberry & Kiwi Tulips

Sweet French crêpes (*crêpes sucrées*) topped with "tulips" made with strawberries and kiwis are like a spring bouquet. For my French husband, Antoine, crêpes are the ultimate comfort food. He makes them once or twice a week for breakfast or for afternoon snacks on the weekends. It's the recipe he knows by heart. I like to have my crêpe with a bit of lemon and sugar, while Antoine has a penchant for a luscious chocolate spread on his. You can also serve them with a dollop of *chantilly* (vanilla-infused whipped cream) instead. Enjoy these comforting crêpes in the way that speaks to you.

MAKES AROUND 8 CRÊPES

FOR THE BATTER
125 g (1 cup) all-purpose flour
2 eggs
300 ml (1¼ cups) milk
1 teaspoon–1 tablespoon sugar, depending on your preferred sweetness
A pinch of salt
1 generous tablespoon (25 g) butter, melted, plus some extra for the pan

FOR THE DECORATION
6–8 strawberries
2 kiwi fruits

TO SERVE
Lemon wedges and granulated sugar, chocolate spread, *or chantilly* (vanilla whipped cream)

To make the batter, place the flour, eggs, milk, sugar, salt and butter in a blender and blend well. Refrigerate the batter for 1 hour.

Heat a non-stick pan over medium-high heat and lightly grease the pan with melted butter. Pour approximately 3 tablespoons of batter into the pan and swirl to spread evenly. Cook for about 30 seconds, then flip and cook 30 seconds more until golden brown.

Cut the tops off the strawberries, then cut them in half. Cut each halved strawberry into four pieces using vertical cuts. Remove one piece, so you can make a tulip shape with 3 vertical-cut pieces.

Peel the kiwi and cut it into thin vertical slices for stems and leaves.

Fold the crêpes twice (into triangles) and place them on plates. Arrange the strawberries and kiwi slices on each crêpe.

Serve according to your preference.

An assortment of cherry tomatoes—
red, orange, and yellow hues in round and
elongated oval forms—resembles the vibrant
colors and shapes of tulips. The following
recipes draw inspiration from this striking
similarity, using cherry tomatoes as the
primary medium to paint a picture of tulips
on your plate. Don't hesitate to experiment
with various shapes, sizes, and colors to
create your very own edible flower bunch.

"Tulip Bouquet" Caprese Salad

Spring is served! Build a tulip bouquet with cherry tomatoes, green beans, mozzarella, and basil leaves. I often opt for this salad as a starter for a spring lunch.

SERVES 4

Cherry tomato medley
(red, orange, yellow), 12 in total
12 mini mozzarella balls
12 green beans, both ends trimmed
24 large basil leaves

With a small paring knife, cut a cross into one end of each cherry tomato, slitting down to about ¾ of the tomato. Scoop out the insides to make room for the mozzarella ball.

Cut the mini mozzarella balls to the size of the cherry tomatoes (I cut them in half) and stuff the tomatoes.

Bring a pot of salted water to a boil and cook the green beans for about 4 minutes, or until just tender but with a little snap. Transfer the cooked green beans to a bowl of ice water to let them cool, then drain.

On a plate, arrange the mozzarella-stuffed cherry tomatoes with green bean stems and basil leaves. Serve with olive oil and balsamic vinegar or your favorite dressing.

Tulip Cherry Tomato & Zucchini Quiche

This zucchini-ricotta quiche, baked with cherry tomatoes and zucchini disguised as tulips, is the perfect centerpiece for a bright and merry spring brunch. Red tulips against golden quiche: the contrast of these primary colors brings fresh and invigorating spring energy to conversations around the table.

MAKES 1 QUICHE (25 CM/9 IN)

1 package of store-bought shortcrust pastry
Olive oil, for sauteing
1 zucchini (make 8 strips of 3 mm/⅛ in width and 5 cm/2 in length for tulip stems; slice the rest into rounds)
1 garlic clove, minced
Salt and pepper, to taste
250 g (1 cup) ricotta, drained for about 1 hour to remove excess water
60 g (2 ounces) Parmigiano Reggiano, grated
3 eggs
125 ml (½ cup) heavy cream
4 cherry tomatoes, halved
Fresh basil leaves

TOOL
Tart tin (25 cm/9 in diameter)

Preheat the oven to 200°C (390°F).

Roll out the store-bought shortcrust pastry and fit it into a buttered tart pan. Press the pastry firmly into the bottom and sides of the pan. Fold in the excess dough around the edge.

Prick the bottom of the crust with a fork. Cover the crust with parchment paper and fill it with pie weights or dried beans or rice.

Bake for 20 minutes, until the edges are lightly golden. Remove from the oven and carefully lift out the parchment paper and pie weights. Bake for another 5–10 minutes and remove from the oven. Set the oven to 180°C (350°F).

Heat the olive oil in a large skillet over medium heat. Add the sliced zucchini and sauté until softened.

Add the minced garlic and cook for one additional minute. Season generously with salt and pepper to taste. Remove from the heat and set aside.

Add a pinch of salt and pepper to the drained ricotta and mix well.

Scatter one third of the grated Parmigiano Reggiano on the par-baked tart, then add the cooked zucchini rounds followed by the ricotta, spreading evenly.

In a medium-sized mixing bowl, whisk together the eggs, heavy cream, and the rest of the grated Parmigiano Reggiano.

Pour the egg mixture into the tart shell, spreading it evenly. Arrange the halved cherry tomatoes and 8 zucchini strips on top, pressing them gently into the mixture, creating tulip shapes. (You can create the tulip blooms by carefully cutting notches in one end of the cherry tomatoes.)

Bake for around 40 minutes or until the filling is set and the top is golden brown. If the pastry edges brown too quickly, cover them with aluminum foil to prevent burning.

Remove the quiche from the oven and let it cool for at least 10 minutes before slicing. Garnish with fresh basil leaves and serve warm or at room temperature.

"Tulip" Pendant Mini Pizzas

Pizza bianca is a perfect canvas for cherry tomatoes and zucchini arranged to remind you of a bouquet of tulips. I've made my mini pizzas in oval shapes to make them look like vintage locket pendants, but you can also make them into little rectangles instead.

——————— MAKES 4 MINI PIZZAS ———————

1 batch of pizza dough
(see recipe p. 31) or use
store-bought pizza dough
(around 250 g)

60 g (¼ cup) ricotta
25 g (¼ cup) grated
Parmigiano Reggiano
35 g mozzarella, grated
A pinch of salt and pepper to taste

Cherry tomato medley
(red, orange, yellow), 8–10 in total
⅓ zucchini
8 basil leaves

TOOL
Oval pastry cutter,
13 x 9 cm/ 5 x 3½ in (optional)

If you are preparing the pizza dough yourself, see the base recipe on p. 31 for instructions. Roll out the dough to your desired thickness. If you are using store-bought dough, take it out of the fridge 15 minutes before preparation. Unpack the dough and unroll it.

Preheat the oven to 200°C (390°F).

Cut the pizza dough into four small ovals with a pastry cutter or into rectangles with a knife.

In a bowl, combine the ricotta, Parmigiano Reggiano, and mozzarella with a pinch of salt and pepper to make the cheese base, then spread the mixture on the dough.

Slice the cherry tomatoes in half and cut out two small triangles at the top to make the cherry tomatoes resemble a tulip. Julienne the zucchini into thin strips (6–8 cm/3–4 in long) for the tulip stems.

Arrange the cherry tomatoes and zucchini strips on the pizzas to make tulip shapes.

Bake for 12–15 minutes until the cheese mixture has melted and the crust is golden brown.

Add basil leaves for the tulip leaves and serve.

Rose

Roses have long been a symbol of enchanted love—the kind that weaves its magic through fairy tales like "Beauty and the Beast."

As a child, I found myself admiring roses from afar, their glamor and imposing presence making them too special to be played with, too grand to disturb.

Unlike daisies, which I transformed into jewelry and playthings, roses remained untouched. Perhaps it was the thorns, acting like noble knights in shining armor, shielding the rose from harm. To me, a rose was the queen of flowers.

Roses continued to remain special into my adulthood. They were always present in my bouquets for celebratory occasions, such as graduations or birthdays, or as tender gestures from boys expressing their feelings. Roses have etched themselves into my memories as emblems of love and appreciation.

Hence, these rose-inspired recipes are created for special romantic occasions: Valentine's Day, a birthday, an anniversary, or a date night. For me, food is a love language. It's through these rose dishes that I say, "I love you, and I consider this moment we spend together very special."

"Rose Petal" Panna Cotta

Light and soft, yet rich and velvety, panna cotta is one of my favorite desserts to serve at the end of dinner. Here is a vanilla panna cotta topped with sliced strawberries arranged to look like rose petals. Served in a long-stemmed coupe, it reminds me of the enchanted rose in the story of Beauty and her Beast, the symbol of true love.

MAKES 4

3 gelatin sheets (5 g in total)
1 vanilla bean
300 ml (1¼ cups) heavy cream
200 ml (generous ¾ cup) milk
50 g (¼ cup) sugar
A pinch of salt

500 g (1 pint) strawberries, washed, dried, and thinly sliced

Soak the gelatin sheets in a bowl of cold water for 5 minutes. Remove them from the bowl and squeeze out excess water before using.

Split the vanilla bean in half lengthwise and scrape the vanilla seeds from the pod with a knife.

In a saucepan, combine the heavy cream, milk, sugar, vanilla seeds, and a pinch of salt and bring to a simmer over low heat.

Remove from the heat, add the softened gelatine sheets, and stir until completely dissolved.

Divide the mixture between 4 coupe glasses and refrigerate until set, at least 3 hours.

Arrange the sliced strawberries on the panna cotta in an arrangement like rose petals and serve.

Strawberry Roses with Whipped Cream

Strawberries transformed into red roses are both the
dessert and the décor for a candlelit table for two.

———————————————— SERVES 2 ————————————————

½ pack (from a 500 g/1 pint pack)
strawberries (8–10 strawberries),
washed and dried with a
paper towel

120 g (½ cup) double cream
or heavy cream
1 tablespoon powdered sugar
¼ teaspoon vanilla extract

TOOLS
Skewer sticks, floral tape,
rose leaves

Gently insert a skewer stick into each
strawberry tip, making sure not to
push all the way through.

Create "petals" by cutting thin slices
out of the bottom, taking care not to
cut all the way through the berry. The
slices should be attached at the base.

Make additional layers until you get to
the top of the strawberry. Repeat this
process with all the berries.

Starting from the top, just beneath
the strawberry, wrap the skewer with
floral tape. The floral tape should
cover the base of the strawberry.

Optional: Add leaves from rose stems.
As you're wrapping, add a few leaves
just under the strawberry and continue
wrapping with floral tape.

Using an electric mixer, whip the
cream with the powdered sugar and
vanilla until soft peaks form.

To serve, place the strawberry roses in
a large vase or small individual vases
and serve with the whipped cream.

Mini "Rose" Apple Pies

Mini apple pies, tinted with hibiscus, boast a rosy hue and look like red roses. Serve them with a scoop of vanilla ice cream and a sprig of mint to give the illusion of a blooming blossom on the plate.

MAKES 8

250 ml (1 cup) water
10 g (¼ cup) dried hibiscus tea
125 ml (½ cup) sugar

3 apples (choose a variety that is suitable for baking)

1 store-bought package of puff pastry
4 tablespoons sugar
2 teaspoons cornstarch
Ground cinnamon (optional)

TOOLS
Flower-shaped cookie cutter (10 cm/4 in)
Muffin tin

Bring the water to a boil and add the hibiscus tea. Let it steep for about 5 minutes, then strain out the hibiscus. The color should be a deep magenta.

Cut the apples in half, remove the core, and slice them thinly. Place the apple slices in the hibiscus tea and simmer for 5–10 minutes, until they are soft and pliable.

Remove the apple slices from the tea and spread them out on paper towels to cool. Gently pat them dry to remove any excess moisture. Keep the poaching liquid.

Once the apples have cooled, gently toss them with 3 tablespoons of sugar and 2 teaspoons of cornstarch until they're evenly coated.

Preheat the oven to 200°C (390°F).

Roll out the puff pastry and use a flower-shaped cookie cutter to cut out as many flower shapes as you can (8 for me). Press each cut-out into the cup of a muffin tin, making sure the pastry goes up the sides.

Sprinkle the hollow of each pastry cup with a bit of the remaining sugar (about 1 tablespoon in total), and a dash of cinnamon, if using.

Arrange the apple slices on a flat surface, overlapping them slightly to create a long line. Starting from one end, roll up the apples to create a rose shape. Place each rose into the hollow of a pastry cup. If there is more space in the pastry cup, add a few more slices to give extra layers and fill the space.

Bake for 30–35 minutes until the pastry is golden brown. If the pastries are browning too quickly, cover them with aluminum foil.

While the pies are baking, prepare the glaze by reducing a mixture of the hibiscus apple-poaching water with ½ cup of sugar. Simmer until the mixture thickens slightly.

Once the pastries are done, remove them from the oven and brush the tops with the hibiscus glaze. Cool them for a few minutes before removing them from the muffin tin. Let them cool completely before serving.

Sunflower

When I was a child, I remember sunflowers
seeming colossal to me, standing tall and
proud with their majestic stature, often taller
than I was. I had to gaze up to admire them,
as though looking up at the sun in the sky.

To be honest, sunflowers weren't my favorites.
They didn't strike me as cute or traditionally
pretty, perhaps due to their size and how
they looked in the garden or field. Their
appearance was somewhere between a
flower and a tree.

However, my perception eventually began
to shift, influenced largely by the sweltering
summers of Korea and Japan. The heat was
intense, and the humidity stifling:
I felt like I was walking into a sauna or being
steamed like a bun in a bamboo basket.
In these moments when everything seemed

about to wilt, sunflowers presented a different narrative. They thrived instead of wilting, their bright yellow petals striking a vibrant contrast under the clear blue summer sky. Their vitality and strength reminded me of summer's positive aspects, nudging me to see that it was still a season I eagerly awaited each year.

Perhaps my vision also shifted because my birthday is in August and, knowing my love for flowers, my friends often presented me with beautiful bouquets. And many times, sunflowers were amongst them, their vibrancy brightening the day, like a big smile.

Over time, these towering, initially intimidating flowers transformed into symbols of hope and excitement, the heralds of sunny days and joyful moments.

Apricot & Blackberry "Sunflower" Galette

These galettes, filled with the summer bounty of fresh apricots and blackberries, conjure up sunflowers. Serve them on a sunny day for dessert or pack them for a picnic near a sunflower field.

MAKES 2 GALETTES (16 CM/6 IN)

FOR THE PIE CRUST
200 g (1½ cups) all-purpose flour
2 tablespoons sugar
½ teaspoon salt
100 g (7 tablespoons) cold butter, cubed
3 tablespoons ice water

FOR THE FILLING
4 tablespoons sugar (adjust to taste)
2 teaspoons cornstarch
¼ teaspoon ground cinnamon (optional)
4–5 apricots (around 200–250 g), sliced
7 blackberries, halved

10 g (scant tablespoon) butter

FOR THE EGG WASH
1 egg
1 tablespoon of water

In a large bowl, mix the flour, sugar, and salt. Add the cold, cubed butter. Using your fingertips, rub the butter into the flour until it resembles coarse breadcrumbs. Gradually add the ice water, a tablespoon at a time, and mix until the dough comes together. Divide the dough in half, shape each half into a disk, wrap them in plastic wrap, and refrigerate for at least 1 hour.

Preheat the oven to 200°C (390°F).

For the filling, in a small bowl, mix the sugar, cornstarch, and optional ground cinnamon. Add 1 tablespoon of the mixture to the blackberries and the rest to the apricots. Toss well to ensure the fruit is evenly coated.

Roll out one of the pie crust disks on a lightly floured surface to a circle of about 20 cm (8 in) in diameter. Leaving about 2 cm (1 in) of border around the edges, arrange the blackberries in the center and the sliced apricots around them to mimic a sunflower. Fold the edges of the pie crust over the filling, pleating as necessary to create a neat circle. Dot the filling with butter. Whisk the egg with 1 tablespoon of water to create an egg wash, and brush the exposed crust with it.

Repeat the process with the second galette.

Bake the galettes for approximately 30 minutes, or until the crust is golden and the filling is bubbly. Let the galette cool before serving.

Mini Okonomiyaki Sunflowers

When I reflect on the summers I've spent in Japan, two images come to mind—sunflowers and *hanabi*, the Firework Festival.

Hanami is the highlight of the spring season, and for summer season it's *Hanabi—hana* (花: flower) and *bi* (火:fire) meaning "fire flower" or fireworks. There's a resemblance between the two: the fireworks burst into life against the dark canvas of the night sky, lighting up the world with dazzling brightness for a few brief moments before fading back into the darkness. It's a spectacle as ephemeral as the blooming cherry blossoms of spring.

So despite the sweltering heat, I found myself going to *hanabi* events year after year. The fun and festive atmosphere, brimming with people (including myself) dressed in colorful *yukata* (lightweight summer kimonos), the plethora of street food stalls, and the joyful gathering of friends that culminated in the fantastic display of fireworks is an experience so spellbinding that it makes one forget all the discomfort of the sultry summer heat.

One dish that is synonymous with these *hanabi* festivals and summer in Japan for me is okonomiyaki, one of the most popular street foods at festivals. Okonomiyaki, translating to "grilled as you like it," is a savory pancake containing a variety of ingredients, such as cabbage, egg, and meat or seafood, topped with okonomiyaki sauce, mayonnaise, and dried bonito flakes. Mini Okonomiyaki Sunflowers are a tribute to the sunflowers and *hanabi* that brought joy and energy to those hot and humid days for me. You'll find a classic okonomiyaki topped with sliced cheese to resemble sunflower petals. But as the name itself suggests (okonomiyaki or "grilled as you like it"), I encourage you to play around and improvise with the ingredients, as you like it.

MAKES 4–5 MINI OKONOMIYAKI (8 CM/3 IN DIAMETER)

FOR THE BATTER
100 g (¾ cup) all-purpose flour
2 teaspoons dashi powder
120 ml (½ cup) water
1 egg
½ teaspoon baking powder

1 tablespoon chopped benishoga
   (pickled red ginger)
50 g green onion (about 1),
   thinly sliced
200 g (7 ounces) cabbage,
   thinly sliced

Bacon or very thin pork strips
   (optional)

FOR THE TOPPING
4–5 slices yellow cheddar cheese
Okonomiyaki sauce
Kewpie mayonnaise

TOOLS
Leaf-shaped cookie cutter
   (2 cm/¾ in)
Squeeze bottle with small nozzle

In a large bowl, mix the flour, dashi powder, water, egg, and baking powder to create a batter.

Heat a griddle, skillet, or oiled frying pan. Immediately before cooking, stir the benishoga, green onions, and cabbage into the batter to ensure they don't get soggy. Using a ladle, pour a ladleful of batter onto the hot surface, making an 8 cm (3 in) pancake, spreading it evenly until it's about 1 cm (¼ in) thick.

If you are using meat, add the bacon or thin pork strips on top of the batter. Cook each side for about 3 minutes or until golden brown.

Cut the cheddar cheese slices with a small leaf-shaped cookie cutter.

Once the okonomiyaki is cooked, smooth about 1 tablespoon of okonomiyaki sauce over the surface using a knife or the back of a spoon, and then using a thin nozzle on the sauce bottle, create cross patterns of Kewpie mayonnaise on top.

Add the leaf-shaped cheese cut-outs around the rim of the pancake to look like yellow sunflower petals, allowing the cheese to melt slightly from the residual heat.

Serve immediately, directly from the griddle, ensuring the okonomiyaki are enjoyed hot.

"Sunflower" Pizza

Garnished with basil leaves, this pizza boasts orange cherry tomatoes and black olives standing in for sunflowers. Serve it as a summer lunch for one or as a shared appetizer with a glass of chilled white or rosé wine.

MAKES 1 PIZZA (24 CM/9 IN)

1 batch of pizza dough
(see recipe p. 31) or use
store-bought pizza dough

60 g (¼ cup) ricotta
25 g (¼ cup) grated
Parmigiano Reggiano
1 small garlic clove, minced
Pinch of salt and pepper

14 oval-shaped, orange
cherry tomatoes
5 basil leaves
4 black olives

OPTIONAL
20 g (1 ounce) mozzarella,
thinly sliced

If you are preparing the pizza dough yourself, see the base recipe on p. 31 for instructions. Roll out the dough to your desired thickness. If you are using store-bought dough, take it out of the fridge 15 minutes before preparation. Unpack the dough and unroll it.

Preheat the oven to 220°C (420°F).

In a bowl, combine the ricotta, Parmigiano Reggiano, garlic, and a pinch of salt and pepper, to taste. Mix well.

Cut the cherry tomatoes in half, so they form oval shapes. Chop the black olives into small pieces.

Lay the pizza dough on a lined baking sheet and pre-bake for about 5 minutes until the dough starts to puff up and turn lightly golden.

Spread the cheese mixture evenly over the pre-baked pizza dough. Place the thinly sliced mozzarella cheese on top (optional).

Arrange the halved cherry tomatoes around the pizza to create a sunflower pattern. Place the chopped black olives at the center of the sunflower pattern.

Bake the pizza for another 10 minutes or until the cheese is melted and bubbly and the crust is golden brown. Remove the pizza from the oven and serve with fresh basil leaves.

"Sunflower" Mango Sticky Rice

Mango sticky rice is one of my favorite desserts from Thailand.
Sweet black sticky rice with flavorful mango, arranged to look
like a sunflower and served with slightly salty coconut sauce,
will remind you of a warm, tropical paradise.

MAKES 4

FOR THE STICKY RICE

250 g (generous 1 cup) rice
  (I used 125 g/½ cup black sticky rice
  and 125 g/½ cup white sticky rice)
200 ml (¾ cup) coconut milk
2 pandan leaves, tied into a knot
75 g (⅔ cup) sugar
¼ teaspoon salt

FOR THE COCONUT SAUCE

100 ml (⅓ cup) coconut milk
1 tablespoon sugar
¼ teaspoon salt
½ teaspoon cornstarch mixed
  with 1 tablespoon water

1–2 tablespoons fried mung
  beans or sesame seeds

4 ripe mangoes

To make the sticky rice, rinse the black and white glutinous rice until the water runs clear. Soak the rice in water for 6–8 hours or overnight.

After soaking, drain the rice. Steam it using a rice steamer for 30–35 minutes, until it is cooked and sticky.

While the rice is steaming, in a small saucepan, combine the coconut milk, pandan leaves, sugar, and salt. Warm the mixture over medium heat until the sugar is fully dissolved.

Once the rice is cooked, transfer it to a large bowl and pour the warm coconut mixture over it. Stir gently to combine. Cover the bowl and let it sit for around 15 minutes to allow the coconut milk mixture to absorb.

To make the coconut sauce, combine the coconut milk, sugar, and salt in a separate saucepan.

Mix the cornstarch with a little bit of water to make a slurry. Add this to the saucepan. Stir the mixture over medium heat until the sugar is fully dissolved and the sauce has thickened slightly.

Assembly: Peel the mangoes and cut them into thin slices. Fan the mango slices around each plate to look like sunflowers petals.

Once the sticky rice is ready, using an ice cream scoop, form the rice into balls and place them at the center of each plate.

Sprinkle the fried mung beans or sesame seeds on top of the rice. Serve with the warm coconut sauce on the side.

"Sunflower" Pineapple & White Chocolate-Glazed Doughnuts

In the art world, sunflowers are synonymous with Vincent van Gogh. The yellow flowers were a source of inspiration for the Dutch artist, who painted them repeatedly. They star in 11 of his works and are present in more as secondary subjects. A visit to The National Gallery in London, where I saw his portrayal of sunflowers, inspired me to create an edible homage: doughnut holes, glazed with white chocolate and topped with dried pineapple slices, like sunflowers in a vase.

MAKES AROUND 25

FOR THE PINEAPPLE SUNFLOWERS
1 ripe pineapple
Cocoa powder for dusting

FOR THE DOUGHNUT HOLES
3.5 g (1 teaspoon) instant dried yeast
17 g (1 tablespoon + 1 teaspoon) sugar
60 ml (¼ cup) lukewarm milk
1 egg
20 g (1½ tablespoons) butter, melted
175 g (1½ cups) all-purpose flour
¼ teaspoon salt
Oil for frying

100 g (3½ ounces) white chocolate, chopped

TOOLS
Round cookie cutter
   (3–4 cm/1–1½ in diameter)
Muffin tin
Small brush
Kitchen thermometer

To make the pineapple sunflowers, preheat the oven to 100°C (210°F).

Cut off the top and bottom of the pineapple. Then stand it upright and carefully slice off the skin, making sure to remove all the "eyes" or brown spots using a melon baller or a teaspoon. Using a very sharp knife or a mandoline, slice the pineapple into very thin rounds (about 2 mm/ ⅒ in or as thin as possible). Pat the pineapple slices dry with a paper towel to remove any excess moisture.

Line 2 baking sheets with parchment paper and arrange the pineapple slices in a single layer. Bake the pineapple slices for 2–3 hours, flipping them halfway through. The goal is to dry the slices until they are golden and mostly dry, but not entirely crisp.

Once baked and while still warm, drape the slices over the upside-down cups of a muffin tin (or use small water glasses). Let the pineapple flowers cool completely.

Using a small brush, dust the center of each dried pineapple with a touch of cocoa powder to make them resemble sunflower centers.

To make the doughnut holes, in a small bowl, add the yeast and 1 teaspoon of sugar to the warm milk. Allow the mixture to sit for about 5–10 minutes until it bubbles up and becomes frothy. In a medium-sized bowl, whisk the egg and melted

butter. Incorporate the yeast mixture and mix well. Stir in the flour, salt, and 1 tablespoon of sugar, and mix until a dough forms and it becomes hard to mix.

Lightly grease a work surface, transfer the dough to the surface, and knead for about 10 minutes until smooth. Cover the dough and let it rise until doubled in size, about 1 hour.

Roll out the dough to about 1 cm (½ in) thickness, and cut it into circles using a round cookie cutter. Cover the doughnut holes and let them rise a second time, for 15–20 minutes.

Heat oil to 170°C (340°F) and fry the dough balls at 160–170°C (320–340°F) for 2–3 minutes until golden brown.

Assembly: Melt the white chocolate in a heatproof metal or glass bowl set over simmering water. Remove from the water once melted.

Dip one side of each doughnut hole in the melted white chocolate and top with a dried pineapple flower. Allow to fully dry.

For presentation, serve these treats with mint leaves on a plate, or make sunflower sticks. To do this, dab a bit of melted white chocolate on the tip of a skewer, attach the pineapple doughnut hole and let the chocolate dry to secure it. Wrap the rest of the stick with floral tape. Display them in a vase like a bouquet of sunflowers.

Other Flowers

"Camellia" Bingsu

Camellias are the roses of winter. Blooming late winter to early spring, they bridge the seasons, greeting us as the first blossoms of the year. Unlike many flowers that shed individual petals, camellias drop the entire bloom intact, looking as if they are blooming again on the ground, creating a display of whole flowers, like a welcoming red carpet.

This camellia bingsu is Korean-style shaved ice (shaved milk ice) topped with grapefruit and orange supremes to resemble a winter camellia. Serve with additional condensed milk on the side for extra sweetness.

SERVES 2

200 ml (¾ cup) milk
50 ml (¼ cup) condensed milk
50 ml (¼ cup) water
2 grapefruits
1 orange

Additional condensed milk
  for serving
Mint leaves to garnish

Combine the milk, condensed milk, and water, then freeze the mixture in an ice cube tray or plastic freezer bag. Ensure the mixture is frozen for at least 5 hours, or better yet, overnight.

Peel and segment the grapefruits and the orange into supremes. Slice the orange supremes into smaller pieces.

Using an ice shaving machine or blender, shave the frozen milk mixture into a small bowl or coupe glass.

Arrange the grapefruit supremes in concentric circles in the cup or bowl, placing the orange pieces in the middle to resemble a camellia flower.

Garnish with fresh mint and serve immediately. Drizzle with additional condensed milk for an extra sweet touch before eating.

Asparagus "Mimosa"

Asparagus Mimosa—a classic French spring dish consisting of lively green asparagus topped with brilliant yellow, finely chopped hard-boiled eggs—is, as its name suggests, a dish that looks akin to blossoming mimosa flowers.

SERVES 4 AS SIDE DISHES

2 eggs
200 g (½ pound) asparagus, tough ends trimmed

FOR THE DRESSING
2 tablespoons white wine vinegar
4 tablespoons olive oil
1 teaspoon honey
1 teaspoon Dijon mustard
Salt and pepper to taste

OPTIONAL
Fresh dill for garnish

Bring a pot of water to a boil. Once boiling, lower the heat to a simmer, carefully add the eggs using a slotted spoon, and cook for 10–11 minutes, or to your desired doneness. After they are hard-cooked, place them in a bowl of ice water to cool. When they are cooled, peel the eggs. Separate the yolks and whites, then dice each.

Bring a large pot of salted water to a boil. Add the asparagus and cook for about 3 minutes (less or more depending on the thickness of the asparagus) until just tender. Drain the asparagus and immediately transfer to a bowl of ice water. Once cooled, drain and pat dry using paper towels.

In a small bowl, whisk together the vinegar, olive oil, honey, and Dijon mustard, or alternatively, combine these ingredients in a jar and shake until well blended. Season the mixture with salt and pepper according to your taste.

Arrange the asparagus on a serving platter. Sprinkle the chopped hard-boiled egg whites first, then the yolks. Garnish with fresh dill to resemble mimosa leaves, and serve with the dressing.

"Water Lily" Onions

This is a dish inspired by my visit to Claude Monet's house and garden in Giverny. More specifically, it is inspired by the water lilies in his vast pond, which he captured in his ethereal paintings. Being there, I really felt like I had just walked into his paintings.

Returning home, I wanted to bring a piece of Monet's world into my kitchen. Alongside a classic French chicken dish taken right from Monet's recipes in *The Monet Cookbook* (Prestel, 2016), I decided to serve Water Lily Onions to capture a taste of French country cooking, paying homage to Monet by painting plates with the flavors and colors inspired by his palette. *Bon appétit!*

SERVES 4 AS SIDE DISHES

4 small or medium onions
   (you can mix red and white)
2 yellow cherry tomatoes, halved
Olive oil
Salt and pepper

Preheat the oven to 200°C (390°F).

Peel the onions and trim the ends so that they sit flat. Use a sharp knife to slice criss-cross across each onion, making 6 or 8 wedges and leaving about 1 cm at the bottom without cutting through.

Bring a large pot of water to a boil, carefully add the onions, and poach them for about 3 minutes.

Remove the onions from the water and once they have cooled, open them up slightly and add a half cherry tomatoes in the middle.

Drizzle with a bit of olive oil and season with salt and pepper to taste. Place on a baking sheet, cover with foil, and bake for 20 minutes, then remove the foil and bake for an additional 10 minutes.

Optional: Serve ungarnished or with basil pesto as a side dish to a meal.

Blooming Rice Paper Chips

Like witnessing the magical moment when flowers bloom, watch rice paper instantly puff up and blossom into beautiful flowers upon frying. Serve as a crunchy snack for your *apéritif* with cheese and charcuterie or place on salads for the extra crunch.

MAKES ABOUT 20

10–20 sheets rice paper
50 g (¼ cup) cooked short grain rice
¼ teaspoon ground turmeric

Oil for frying
Salt and seasoning

TOOL
Kitchen thermometer

Using kitchen scissors, cut the rice paper into flower shapes (with 6–8 petals, as preferred). Make two sizes, the bigger ones around 8 cm (3 in) in diameter and smaller ones around 5 cm (2 in) in diameter.

Place the cooked rice in a small bowl, add the turmeric, and mix well to color the rice yellow.

Using a bit of cooked rice as "glue," place the smaller rice paper shape on the bigger rice paper shape and press it down. Top it with more yellow rice.

Dry the flowers by air drying or dehydrating them in an oven. (I like to dry them in a 70°C (160°F) oven for about 30 minutes).

Fill a pan with 1-2 cm/½ to ¾ in of oil and heat it until it reaches 180°C (350°F). Fry the assembled flowers in the oil for a few seconds until they puff up.

Season with salt or your favorite seasoning.

Bee

There are many ways to welcome spring in nature with our senses. With our eyes, we see vibrant green leaves and carpets of colorful flowers. With our nose, we smell gentle floral aromas. With our ears, we hear birds chirping and bees buzzing as they get busy collecting nectar. The latter is for me the defining sound of spring, a bustling hum that fills gardens, parks, and meadows.

Spring's ensemble of sensory experiences is exemplified by the interplay between flowers and bees. The bond between bees and flowers is profound. More than a simple partnership, it's a tale of lovers intertwined in a symbiotic relationship, flowers providing nectar to nourish the bees, and bees pollinating the flowers in return, helping them to reproduce. Without this relationship, we would have no flowers, fruits, vegetables and, of course, honey.

By dedicating a selection of recipes to bees, I wanted to celebrate this captivating love story in nature.

Bees and Flowers Canapés

Mini mozzarella balls, cherry tomatoes, and black olives are sliced
and arranged to look like little bees and flowers. Serve these
miniatures on crackers to make canapés or on toast with
a bit of basil pesto for spring gatherings.

———— MAKES 16 PIECES (8 BEES AND 8 FLOWERS) ————

16 crackers of your choice

FOR THE BEES
2 yellow or orange oval-shaped
   cherry tomatoes
2 pitted black olives
1 black pitted olive for
   "antennae" (optional)
1 mini mozzarella ball

FOR THE FLOWERS
4 round, yellow cherry tomatoes
8 mini mozzarella balls

OPTIONAL
Basil leaves

To make the bee canapés, cut
2 orange cherry tomatoes and 2 black
olives in half lengthwise. Then cut
each half into 4 thin slices.

On a cracker, arrange the thin slices
of cherry tomato and black olive
alternately to create the bee's body
and stripes.

Optional: For the antennae, cut a
black olive into thin rings. Then cut
these rings in half to make small
semi-circles. Arrange two of these
pieces at the rounded end of the
bee's body.

Cut a mini mozzarella ball into
5–6 thin, round slices. Then trim off
the edges to create a wing shape.
Place two "wings" on either side of
the bee's body.

To make the flower canapés, cut
each mini mozzarella ball into
5–6 round slices.

Cut the yellow cherry tomatoes
in half.

On a cracker, arrange the round
mozzarella slices in a circle to form
flower petals. Place the halved yellow
cherry tomato at the center of the
mozzarella circle to complete the
flower.

Add basil leaves around the flowers
and bees and serve.

Tamago Bee Sushi

Tamago sushi (卵寿司), which translates to egg sushi, is sushi rice
topped with sliced omelet and wrapped with a strip of nori seaweed.
By adding another strip of nori and wings of thinly sliced radish
(as Japanese egg rolls are traditionally served with grated radish),
you can transform this tamago sushi into little bees. Serve with soy sauce
for dipping and a bowl of miso soup for an enjoyable meal.

FOR THE SUSHI RICE
200 g (¾ cup) cooked short
   grain sushi rice
½ tablespoon rice vinegar
½ teaspoon sugar
⅛ teaspoon salt

FOR THE OMELET
3 eggs
½ tablespoon tsuyu
½ tablespoon water
1 nori sheet
¼ daikon radish (100–150 g)

TOOLS
Tamagoyaki rectangular pan
Leaf-shaped cookie cutter
   (around 2.5 cm/1 in)

To make the sushi rice, in a small bowl, combine the rice vinegar, sugar, and salt and stir until the sugar dissolves.

Transfer the cooked sushi rice to a large bowl and pour the vinegar mixture over the rice. Using a rice paddle or spoon, gently fold the vinegar mixture into the rice until well combined, and let it cool to room temperature. Take a small amount of cooled sushi rice (around 18 g or 2 tablespoons) and shape it into an oval. Repeat. (You should have 10–11 ovals.)

To make the omelet, combine the eggs, tsuyu, and water in a bowl, whisking until thoroughly mixed.

Place a tamagoyaki pan over medium-low heat and use a paper towel to apply a thin layer of cooking oil to the surface. Pour a small amount of the egg mixture into the pan, ensuring it spreads evenly by tilting the pan. When the bottom of the egg has set but the top is still slightly runny, use two spatulas to roll the egg toward you, creating a small roll.

Push the roll to the far end of the pan and pour another thin layer of the egg mixture so it covers the remaining surface of the pan (and slides under the roll). When the new layer has set but the top is still slightly runny, repeat the gesture of rolling the existing egg roll toward you. It will pick up more layers as it rolls.

Repeat the process until you have used up all of the egg mixture. When the omelet is fully cooked, remove it from the pan and let it cool for a few minutes.

Slice the roll to 1 cm (⅓ in) thickness (it will yield around 10–11 pieces).

To assemble, place a slice of omelet atop the ovals of rice.

Using kitchen scissors, cut strips of seaweed (nori) to around 1 cm (⅓ in) thickness and 10 cm (4 in) length, creating 2 for each sushi piece, so 20–22 strips total. Fold 2 strips around the sushi to hold it together and also to create the bee's striped pattern.

Thinly slice the daikon radish (around 2 mm/1/16 in) and cut it into oval wing shapes using a knife or a small, leaf-shaped cookie cutter.

Top each piece of sushi with two slices of radish to create wings and serve.

Almond Croissant with Flowers and Bees

Here is a spring makeover for day-old croissants! Brush each croissant
with vanilla syrup, fill and top with almond paste, bake until golden,
and finally top with almond "bees" and "flowers."

SERVES 6

6 croissants
   (preferably day-old croissants)

FOR THE VANILLA SYRUP
250 ml (1 cup) water
250 g (1¼ cups) sugar
1 vanilla bean

*Note: For this recipe, you will use
1 tablespoon of the vanilla syrup for
each croissant, so around 6 tablespoons in all. Set the rest aside to use
for the "Cherry" Raspberry-Vanilla
Cake on p. 116.*

FOR THE ALMOND CREAM
1 egg
50 g (¼ cup) sugar
50 g (¼ cup) ground almonds
¼ teaspoon salt
50 g (3½ tablespoons) butter,
   softened

FOR THE ALMOND BEES AND FLOWERS
12 chocolate-covered almonds (or dip
   almonds in melted dark chocolate)
40 thinly sliced almonds for flowers
24 thinly sliced almonds for bees

TOOL
Yellow deco melt/icing pen

Preheat the oven to 175°C (350°F).

To make the vanilla syrup, combine
the water and sugar in a small saucepan. Split the vanilla bean lengthwise
and scrape out the seeds. Add both
the seeds and the pod to the saucepan. Place the saucepan over medium
heat and stir until the sugar dissolves
completely. Bring the mixture to a
gentle simmer and cook for about
5 minutes, then remove from heat.
Allow the vanilla syrup to cool slightly
before removing the vanilla pod.

To make the almond cream, in a
medium bowl, mix together the egg,
sugar, ground almonds, salt, and
softened butter until well combined.

Using a knife, carefully slice each
croissant in half horizontally, without
cutting all the way through, leaving
a hinge on one side. Using a brush,
soak both inside surfaces with vanilla
syrup. Spread a generous amount of
almond cream onto the bottom half
of each croissant. Gently close the
croissants and add another layer of
almond cream on top.

Bake the croissants on a lined baking
tray for 15 minutes, or until they are
golden brown and the almond cream
has set. Remove the croissants from
the oven and allow them to cool
slightly on the baking sheet.

To make the almond bees and flowers,
using the deco pen, add yellow
stripes to each chocolate covered
almond and affix two thin almond
slices to create wings. Use five thin
almond slices to create flower "petals"
and "glue" them together in the middle with the yellow deco pen.

Once the croissants have cooled,
add the almond bees and flowers,
using the deco pen as "glue."

Miso Butter Bees

Miso butter—white miso paste simply mixed with softened butter—makes a wonderful condiment, bursting with umami flavor. I've shaped my little butter patties into bees with nori strips and tiny wings. Watch these bees slide (or fly!) down a hot steamed, baked, or grilled potato or ear of corn. You can also serve them on a board with flower-shaped cut-out butter pieces (made using a cookie cutter) at breakfast with toast and fried or scrambled eggs for a cute spring scene at your table.

———————————— MAKES ABOUT 10 PIECES ————————————

15 g (1 tablespoon) white miso
50 g (3½ tablespoons) butter, softened
15 g (1 tablespoon) cold butter
1 nori sheet

TOOL
1 cm (½ in) heart-shaped cookie cutter

Mix the white miso into the softened butter until well incorporated. Lay out a piece of plastic wrap on your countertop and spoon the miso butter mixture onto the plastic wrap. Fold the plastic wrap over the butter, then roll it up, twisting the ends to seal it like a candy wrapper, shaping the butter into a 3 cm (1 in) oval-shaped log. Refrigerate the butter log until firm. Then slice the butter log into 5 mm (⅕ in) slices.

Slice the cold butter into 5 mm (⅕ in) slices as well, and cut it into hearts using the heart-shaped cookie cutter.

Cut each heart in half to create wings. Then add wings to each oval-shaped slice of miso butter by gently pressing them together.

Cut out thin nori strips using kitchen scissors to add bee details (stripes, antennae).

Serve with steamed or baked corn, potatoes, or whatever inspires you.

Cherry

Seeing a ruby-red cherry reminds me of the cheerful mood of early summer days. When I lived in California for a few years, I remember repeatedly asking my parents if we could go cherry picking. It wasn't an activity that I could do year-round. From late May to the end of June was the only time we could enjoy this excursion. I know that's what made cherry picking so special. Upon arriving at the orchard, I was given a bucket, but I remember it took a while for me to fill it up, as I was busy filling my mouth with fruit as I picked. I still remember the burst of warm, juicy, sweet,

California-sun-kissed cherries popping in my mouth and the pure joy I got from them. Going home, my fingertips and lips were stained red with cherry bliss.

Cherries, along with other stone fruit like peaches, apricots, plums, and nectarines, are the fruits of summer. But they offer a slightly different experience from their cousins. They are mini doses of delight in the early season that make you look forward to the euphoria of ripe peaches to come.

"Cherry" Pizza

Just like the warmth and sweetness of sun-kissed cherries bursting in your mouth, the cherry tomatoes on this pizza will give you a wonderful sensation. They join zucchini and basil leaves to disguise themselves as cherries.

MAKES 1 PIZZA (24 CM/9 IN)

1 batch of pizza dough
    (see recipe p. 31) or use
    store-bought pizza dough

60 g (¼ cup) ricotta
25 g (¼ cup) grated Parmigiano
    Reggiano
1 small garlic clove, minced
A pinch of salt and pepper

7 cherry tomatoes
⅓ zucchini
7 basil leaves

If you are preparing the pizza dough yourself, see the base recipe on p. 31 for instructions. Roll out the dough to your desired thickness. If you are using store-bought dough, take it out of the fridge 15 minutes before preparation. Unpack the dough and unroll it.

Preheat the oven to 220°C (425°F).

In a medium-sized bowl, combine the ricotta, Parmigiano Reggiano, and garlic with a pinch of salt and pepper to make the cheese base. Halve the cherry tomatoes and julienne the zucchini into thin strips (4–5 cm/1½–2 in long).

Pre-bake the dough in the oven for 5 minutes.

Take the pizza from the oven, cover it with the cheese mixture and arrange the tomatoes and zucchini strips on top to make cherry patterns.

Bake for 10 minutes, or until the cheese mixture has melted and the crust is golden brown. Before serving, add basil leaves as the cherry leaves.

Cherry Tomato Focaccia

I've placed these look-alikes onto a rectangular focaccia so that everyone can get a cute "cherry" on their slice. Serve with a burrata or mozzarella ball and prosciutto on the side for an *apéritif* or as a starter.

MAKES ONE FOCACCIA (SERVES 6)

FOR THE DOUGH
3.5 g (1 teaspoon) dry yeast
1 teaspoon sugar
160 ml (1⅓ cups) lukewarm water
    (mix two parts cold water with
    one part hot water)
250 g (2 cups) flour,
    Tipo 00 or pizza flour
A pinch of salt
Extra-virgin olive oil

FOR THE TOPPINGS
12 cherry tomatoes
½ zucchini
6–12 basil leaves (depending on
    whether you want one leaf or
    two leaves per cherry)

Combine the yeast, sugar, and lukewarm water in a bowl. Mix well and wait for 5–10 minutes until bubbles form.

In a large bowl, place the flour, salt, and ½ tablespoon of olive oil. Pour the yeast mixture into the flour mixture and stir until well combined. Once the dough becomes hard to mix with a spoon, knead for about 10 minutes. Cover the dough and let it proof for about 1 hour at room temperature (or overnight in the fridge).

Once proofed, transfer the dough onto a lightly floured work surface.

Shape the focaccia into a rectangle. Make dimples with your knuckles, and drizzle with 1 tablespoon of olive oil. Cover the focaccia and proof for another 45 minutes.

Preheat the oven to 200°C (390°F).

Julienne the zucchini into thin strips 4–5 cm (1½–2 in) long.

Once the second proof is done, create cherry patterns by placing the cherry tomatoes and zucchini strips on the dough. Sprinkle with salt and bake for 20–25 minutes until golden brown.

Once out of the oven, drizzle with more olive oil and cool for at least 10 minutes. Add basil leaves before serving to complete the cherry patterns.

"Cherry" Raspberry-Vanilla Cake

Fresh raspberries and mint leaves masquerade as cherries on a genoise cake layered with vanilla syrup and mascarpone cream.

Layer cakes often connote special occasions, like birthdays. They demand a bit more effort than other desserts: mastering the genoise, whipping the cream, and carefully assembling the cake layers with their surrounding frosting. Yet, when complete, they truly take center stage. Their visual appeal makes any day feel extraordinary. That's why I enjoy making them from time to time, even without a specific occasion to justify a cake. Dotted with "cherries," this one brings me the joy and excitement of early summer days on top of it all.

RECIPE ON THE NEXT PAGE

FOR THE GENOISE
3 eggs (150 g in total)
80 g (scant ½ cup) sugar
1 teaspoon vanilla extract
25 g (2 tablespoons) butter
20 g (1¼ tablespoons) milk
80 g (⅔ cup) all-purpose flour
A pinch of salt

2–3 tablespoons Vanilla Syrup
   (see the Almond Croissant with
   Flowers and Bees recipe, p. 102)

FOR THE WHIPPED MASCARPONE CREAM
300 g (1¼ cup) mascarpone
300 ml (1¼ cup) heavy cream
60 g (½ cup) powdered sugar
1 teaspoon vanilla extract

200 g fresh raspberries
   (set aside about 10 for decoration)
10 mint sprigs

TOOLS
Cake tin (16 cm/6 in diameter)
Kitchen thermometer

To make the genoise, preheat the oven to 165°C (325°F). Line a 16 cm/6 in diameter cake pan with parchment paper.

In a metal bowl, whisk together the eggs, sugar, and vanilla extract. Heat this mixture over boiling water (the bowl should not touch the water) until the egg temperature is between 38–40°C (100–104°F).

Remove the bowl from the heat. Use a stand or hand mixer to whip the mixture until it triples in size and becomes pale and thick enough to draw a ribbon.

In a separate bowl, combine the butter and milk and heat them over simmering water until fully melted. Set aside.

Sift the flour and salt into the egg mixture. Mix gently until no traces of flour remain. Remove about one cup of batter and mix it into the warm butter and milk mixture. Fold this combination back into the remaining batter.

Carefully pour the batter into the prepared cake tin. Tap the tin against the countertop a few times to remove any air bubbles.

Bake for 30–35 minutes, or until a toothpick inserted comes out clean.

When the genoise is done, flip it onto a cooling rack. Let it cool completely before slicing it horizontally into two equal portions.

To make the whipped mascarpone cream, whip together the mascarpone and vanilla extract in a medium-sized bowl until smooth.

In a large bowl, whip the heavy cream and powdered sugar with a hand or stand mixer until stiff peaks form. Carefully fold the mascarpone mixture into the whipped cream.

To assemble, brush the vanilla syrup on one half of the genoise and then spread a layer of whipped cream. Add fresh raspberries and cover with another layer of cream. Finally, top with the second layer of genoise.

Coat the outside of the cake with cream, chill in the fridge for about 10 minutes, and then apply a second coat of cream.

Decorate the cake with fresh raspberries and mint to make cherry patterns.

Mascarpone & Raspberry "Cherry" Croissant

There are days when I crave something a tad luxurious for breakfast.
That's when I choose to indulge in this decadence: a croissant with
a spread of vanilla mascarpone cream and fresh raspberries.
Little "cherries" are a bonus, a cute and playful touch that elicits
a smile at a glance.

MAKES 2

2 fresh croissants

FOR THE MASCARPONE CREAM
100 ml (⅓ cup) heavy cream
20 g (⅛ cup) powdered sugar
½ teaspoon vanilla extract
100 g (⅓ cup) mascarpone

12 raspberries
A handful of mint leaves
    (big and small, ideally)

In a medium bowl, beat the mascarpone until smooth.

In a separate bowl, combine the heavy cream, powdered sugar, and vanilla extract, and whip until stiff peaks form. Fold the whipped cream into the mascarpone and gently mix until well combined.

Cut 1–2 mint leaves into strips. These will form the cherry stems.

Slice the croissant in half and spread the mascarpone cream on the bottom half. Top with raspberries and mint leaves to create the cherry pattern.

Serve immediately with the top half next to it, so you can see the cherry pattern.

Red Currant
"Cherry" Cream Buns

From cream buns in England to *maritozzi* in Italy, *cream pan* in
Japan and Korea, and other names in many other countries, these
delicious variations of brioche filled with cream are always a delight.
My version is a fusion of these classics with a summery touch:
a brioche bun stuffed with a red berry (red currant and raspberry)
whipped cream and topped with red currants and mint that want
you to see them as mini cherries—a sweet and refreshing treat
with a cherry on top.

──────── MAKES 6 ────────

FOR THE RED BERRY JELLY
200 g (about 1½ cups) raspberries
100 g (1 cup) red currants (set aside
    around 12 berries for decoration)
150 g (¾ cup) sugar
1 teaspoon lemon juice

FOR THE BUNS
30 g (2½ tablespoons) sugar
1 teaspoon instant yeast
150 ml (½ cup) milk, warm
300 g (2½ cups) all-purpose flour
½ teaspoon salt
1 egg
30 g (2 tablespoons) butter, softened

FOR THE RED BERRY CREAM
100–150 g (½–¾ cup) of red berry jelly
    (more or less depending on your
    preferred berry flavor intensity)
50 g (¼ cup) mascarpone
300 ml (1¼ cup) heavy cream.

OR FOR A CLASSIC VANILLA CREAM,
REPLACE WITH
300 ml (1¼ cup) heavy cream
50 g (¼ cup) mascarpone
50 g (¼ cup) sugar
½ teaspoon vanilla extract

FOR THE DECORATION
12 red currant berries
Sprigs of mint
Powdered sugar (optional)

To make the red berry jelly, combine all the ingredients in a saucepan. Cook over medium heat for about 20 minutes, or until the mixture has reduced to a jam-like consistency.

Once the fruit mixture has thickened, pass it through a mesh sieve and discard the pulp. You should end up with about 150 g (½ cup) of strained jelly mixture. Chill in the fridge for several hours or overnight.

To make the buns combine 1 teaspoon of sugar, the yeast and warm milk in a small bowl, and let the mixture sit for about 5–10 minutes, until frothy.

In a large bowl, combine the flour, remaining sugar, and salt.

Add the yeast mixture and egg to the dry ingredients. Mix until a rough dough forms and then knead for about 10 minutes, until the dough is smooth and elastic. Add the softened butter and continue kneading until the butter is incorporated.

Place the dough in a greased bowl, cover it with plastic wrap or a kitchen towel, and let it rise in a warm area until it has doubled in size (1–2 hours).

Punch down the dough, divide it into 6 small pieces, and shape each piece into a bun.

Place the shaped dough on a baking sheet lined with parchment paper, leaving space between each piece. Cover and let the dough rise again until it has increased 1.5 times in size (40 minutes to 1 hour).

Preheat the oven to 180°C (350°F).

Bake the buns for 13–15 minutes or until golden brown.

To make the red berry cream, retrieve the cooled red berry jelly from the fridge—it should have a jelly-like consistency. In a medium-sized bowl, whip the jelly with a whisk until it becomes smooth and spreadable. Add the mascarpone to the whipped jam and mix until well combined.

In a separate bowl, whip the heavy cream with a stand or hand mixer until soft peaks form. Fold the whipped cream into the mascarpone and jam mixture and whip more to incorporate.

To assemble, slice the buns in half, making sure that they are not cut all the way through. Fill the crevice with red berry cream using a piping bag or spoon. Decorate the stripe of red berry cream with red currants and mint leaves to create tiny cherries. Optionally, dust one half of the bun with powdered sugar.

Fruit

The word "fruit" originates from the Latin *fructus*, which gestures at "enjoyment" and "pleasure." *Fructus* is the noun form of the verb *fruor* which means "I enjoy, I derive pleasure from," which I believe perfectly represents the essence of fruits. Historically, and even today, unlike grains, proteins, or vegetables which were a necessary staple of our diets, fruits were considered a rarity— the sweet little luxuries of life.

To me, there's nothing quite like the joy of savoring fruits, especially in the summer months. The height of warm weather brings with it an abundance of these little delights, each with its allure.

For instance, there is something decadent about grapes. Sitting in the shade on a summer afternoon, when I pop the juicy, sweet spheres into my mouth, I feel like the ancient Romans and Greeks depicted in historical paintings, like Thomas Couture's *The Romans in Their Decadence*. I feel a sense of hedonistic glee, almost as though Bacchus or Dionysus himself had blessed these fruits.

I always considered watermelon to be the king of summer fruits, especially in the sweltering Korean summers. Biting into a chilled slice of watermelon brought immediate, cool relief, extinguishing the sun's fiery heat. Then there's the peach. The euphoric moment of biting into a perfectly ripe peach, for me, is one of summer's highlights.

These three fruits have always been my faithful summer companions: by the pool, in the garden, beautifully displayed in a fruit bowl, or tucked into a picnic basket, offering a piece of summertime joy.

I think this is why fruit shapes and patterns make me happy. Each iconic fruit shape—fun, playful, and uniquely identifiable by its forms and colors—reminds me of those summer treats. *Fruor fructus*—I enjoy and derive pleasure from fruit.

Burrata and Blueberry "Grape" Salad

Blueberries, carefully stacked with a small sprig of mint, create a playful imitation of miniature grape clusters—a fun addition to a burrata salad. Serve with a simple dressing of olive oil, honey, and lemon juice to enhance their flavors. Alternatively, if you prefer something sweet, simply serve them with honey on toast.

SERVES 2–4

4 mini burratas
120 g (a generous ½ cup) blueberries, washed and dried
4 sprigs of mint

FOR THE DRESSING
2 tablespoons olive oil
2 tablespoon lemon juice
1 tablespoon honey
A pinch of salt

On a plate, carefully arrange approximately 20 blueberries in a grape-like cluster. Repeat with the remaining blueberries to create 4 grape clusters. Garnish with fresh mint leaves.

Arrange the mini burratas around the plate.

For the dressing, combine the olive oil, lemon juice, honey, and pinch of salt, to taste. Stir until well mixed.

Serve the salad with the honey-lemon dressing on the side (or honey).

Blueberry-Lemon "Grape" Cake

Blueberry and lemon, apple and cinnamon, strawberry and rhubarb—these are classic pairings that complement one another beautifully, each duo bringing out the best in its partner. Blueberry-lemon is one of my favorite combinations, and I especially love it for a cake. This Blueberry-Lemon "Grape" Cake is a vanilla genoise layered with blueberry-lemon compote encased in a cream cheese frosting and decorated with fresh blueberries and mint leaves as "grapes." It's sweet and tangy, rich yet light.

—————— MAKES 1 CAKE (16 CM/6 IN DIAMETER) ——————

FOR THE BLUEBERRY-LEMON COMPOTE
200 g (1 cup) blueberries
2 tablespoons lemon juice
50 g (¼ cup) sugar
1 teaspoon cornstarch

FOR THE GENOISE
3 eggs (150 g/5.29 ounces in total)
80 g (scant ½ cup) sugar
1 teaspoon vanilla extract
25 g (2 tablespoons) butter
20 g (1¼ tablespoons) milk
80 g (⅔ cup) all-purpose flour
A pinch of salt

FOR THE CREAM CHEESE FROSTING
300 g (1½ cup) cream cheese
60 g (½ cup) powdered sugar
1 teaspoon vanilla extract
300 ml (1¼ cup) heavy cream

FOR THE DECORATION
100 g (½ cup) blueberries
Mint leaves

TOOLS
Cake tin (16 cm/6 in diameter)
Kitchen thermometer

To make the blueberry-lemon compote, combine all the ingredients in a small saucepan. Cook the mixture over medium heat for about 10 minutes, until it reaches a jam-like consistency.

To make the genoise, preheat the oven to 165°C (325°F). Line a 16 cm/6 in diameter cake pan with parchment paper.

In a metal bowl, whisk together the eggs, sugar, and vanilla extract. Heat this mixture over boiling water (the bowl should not touch the water) until the temperature is between 38–40°C (100–104°F). Remove the bowl from the heat. Use a stand or hand mixer to whip the mixture until it triples in size and becomes pale and thick enough to draw a ribbon.

Combine the butter and milk and heat them over simmering water until warm and fully melted. Set this aside.

Sift the flour and salt into the egg mixture. Mix gently until no traces of flour remain. Remove about one cup of batter and mix it into the warm butter and milk mixture. Fold this combination back into the remaining batter.

Carefully pour the batter into the prepared cake tin. Tap the tin against the countertop a few times to remove any air bubbles.

Bake for 30–35 minutes, or until a toothpick inserted comes out clean.

When the genoise is done, flip it onto a cooling rack. Let it cool completely before slicing it horizontally into three equal portions.

To make the cream cheese frosting, whip together the cream cheese, vanilla extract, and powdered sugar in a medium-sized bowl until smooth.

In a separate large bowl, whip the heavy cream with a stand mixer until stiff peaks form. Carefully fold the cream cheese mixture into the whipped cream.

To layer, begin with a slice of genoise, then spread half of the blueberry-lemon compote over it, followed by a layer of the cream cheese frosting.

Repeat this process for the second layer, topping it with the third layer of genoise.

Coat the outside of the cake with cream cheese frosting, chill it in the fridge for 10 minutes, and then apply a second coating of frosting.

Decorate the cake with fresh blueberries to resemble grape clusters, and garnish with mint leaves.

"Watermelon" Pizza

Sliced zucchini and tomatoes are assembled in the shape
of watermelon slices to create watermelon-patterned pizza bianca.
Serve as an appetizer for a summer barbecue with frosty, refreshing
beverages alongside.

MAKES 1 PIZZA (24 CM/9 IN)

1 batch of pizza dough
   (see recipe p. 31) or use
   store-bought pizza dough

60 g (¼ cup) ricotta
25 g (¼ cup) grated Parmigiano
   Reggiano
1 small garlic clove, minced
Pinch of salt and pepper

½ zucchini
1 small- to medium-sized tomato
Black sesame seeds

OPTIONAL
20 g (1 ounce) mozzarella,
   thinly sliced

If you are preparing the pizza dough yourself, see the base recipe on p. 31 for instructions. Roll out the dough to your desired thickness. If you are using store-bought dough, take it out of the fridge 15 minutes before preparation. Unpack the dough and unroll it.

Preheat the oven to 220°C (420°F).

In a bowl, combine the ricotta, Parmigiano Reggiano, garlic, and a pinch of salt and pepper to taste. Mix well.

Slice the tomato to about 5 mm (⅛ in) thickness and cut it in half to form semi-circles. Slice the zucchini to the same thickness. Scoop out the interior of the zucchini slices with a spoon so that they fit against the outside curve of the tomatoes.

Make 7–8 watermelons out of the tomato and zucchini semi-circles.

Lay the pizza dough on a lined baking sheet and pre-bake for about 5 minutes, until the dough begins to puff up and turn lightly golden.

Remove from the oven and spread the cheese mixture evenly over the pre-baked pizza dough. Place the thinly sliced mozzarella on top (optional).

Arrange the watermelon pieces across the pizza, adding black sesame for the "watermelon seeds."

Bake the pizza for another 10 minutes or until the cheese is melted and bubbly and the crust is golden brown. Serve immediately.

Watermelon Cucumber Salad

Here is a classic summer salad with a visual twist: miniature watermelon slices made from cucumber and watermelon, with black sesame seeds.

───────────────── SERVES 1 ─────────────────

½ cucumber
¼ watermelon
¼ small red onion
25 g (1 ounce) feta
Black sesame seeds
A sprig of mint leaves

FOR THE DRESSING
Olive oil, lemon or lime juice
Salt and pepper

Cut the cucumber in half lengthwise and scoop out the seeds with a spoon. Then slice the cucumber into 0.5 cm (¼ in) thick slices.

Slice the watermelon to the same thickness and cut the slices into half-moon shapes so that they fit into the inner curve of the cucumber slices.

Thinly slice the red onion and cut the feta into small cubes.

In a bowl, whisk the olive oil, lemon or lime juice, and salt and pepper for the dressing.

Arrange the watermelon, cucumber, red onion, and feta on a plate. Add black sesame seeds to create watermelon "seeds." Add mint leaves and serve with the dressing.

"Fruit Salad" Pizza

Like a fruit salad, this pizza bianca brings together a mélange of the season's most bountiful produce on a pizza. It's topped with my favorite summer "fruits": cherries, peaches, and watermelons, created with tomatoes, zucchini, and basil leaves.

MAKES 1 PIZZA (24 CM/9 IN)

1 batch of pizza dough
   (see recipe p. 31) or use
   store-bought pizza dough

60 g (¼ cup) ricotta
25 g (1 ounce) grated Parmigiano
   Reggiano
Pinch of salt and pepper
1 small garlic clove, minced

½ zucchini
1 small- to medium-sized tomato
3 cherry tomatoes

8 small basil leaves
Black sesame seeds

OPTIONAL
20 g (1 ounce) mozzarella cheese,
   thinly sliced

If you are preparing the pizza dough yourself, see the base recipe on p. 31 for instructions. Roll out the dough to your desired thickness. If you are using store-bought dough, take it out of the fridge 15 minutes before preparation. Unpack the dough and unroll it.

Preheat the oven to 220°C (420°F).

In a bowl, mix the ricotta, Parmigiano Reggiano, garlic, pinch of salt, and pepper until well combined.

Cut the tomato into three slices, with a thickness of about 5 mm (⅕ in), maintaining the curved outer layers whole (these will represent peaches), and cutting the middle layer in half (these will be the watermelons).

Slice a piece of zucchini to match the thickness of the tomato slices. Cut it in half and use a spoon to hollow out the middle so it can accommodate the tomato slices.

Thinly slice the remaining zucchini (to create 6 stems for the cherries).

Cut the cherry tomatoes in half.

Spread the pizza dough on a lined baking sheet and pre-bake for 5 minutes or until the dough begins to puff up and turn a light golden color.

Evenly spread the cheese mixture over the pre-baked pizza dough. If desired, add a layer of thinly sliced mozzarella on top.

Arrange the "fruit" pieces on the pizza and sprinkle black sesame seeds on the "watermelon" slices to resemble seeds. (In total, you should have components to make 3 cherries, 2 watermelons, and 2 peaches.)

Continue baking the pizza for another 10 minutes, or until the cheese is melted and bubbly and the crust is golden brown.

Remove the pizza from the oven, garnish with basil leaves to represent leaves on the cherries and peaches, and serve immediately.

Fish

Longer days and warmer weather mean summer has arrived. I think the best part of summer is its idleness. It's okay to be lazy: no need to rush or think about productivity. As a child, with time off from school, I felt I had all the time in the world, endless hours to play outdoors under skies so blue. Summer's relaxed atmosphere invites a carefree spirit of spontaneity. With no homework to do, we could go on adventures with a light heart. Boundaries between day and night blurred, and the concept of days and weeks faded.

In summer, I got lost in time playing with fish in the water. Like many other kids, my brother and I loved playing in water of any kind, whether sea, lake, stream, or creek. Each place offered different opportunities to see fish. In creeks and streams, we looked for little fish swimming downstream. We chased them, sometimes dipping in a small net in an attempt to catch them. Snorkeling in the ocean, we discovered a whole new world underwater. The best part was swimming with fish, feeling like one of them. I would also accompany my dad, who fished from the pier; I peacefully waited with popsicles or snacks in my hand and the hope of glimpsing a catch.

Spending time with fish was fun. With their variety of sizes, colors, shapes, and patterns, they were a discovery almost every time, like meeting a new friend from a different world. Their fluid and graceful movement as they glide through their tranquil underwater realm resembles those idyllic summer days—effortless and serene. That is what summer is all about.

Fish-Scale Peach Galette

I love making galettes. They are easy, forgiving, and versatile and allow for a variety of shapes to be formed without the need for a tool. This peach galette is an example: create a fish shape you like by simply cutting the pie dough, then arrange peaches for fish scales.

———————— MAKES 1 GALETTE ————————

FOR THE PIE CRUST
200 g (1⅔ cups) all-purpose flour
100 g (7 tablespoons) cold butter, cubed
2 tablespoons sugar
½ teaspoon salt
3 tablespoons ice water

FOR THE FILLING
3 medium-sized peaches, pitted
2–3 tablespoons sugar
1 tablespoon cornstarch
½ teaspoon ground cinnamon

10 g (1 scant tablespoon) butter
1 chocolate chip

FOR THE EGG WASH
1 egg, whisked
1 tablespoon water

In a food processor, pulse the flour, butter, sugar, and salt until crumbly. Add the water one tablespoon at a time until the mixture comes together as a dough. Form the dough into an oval, wrap in plastic wrap, and chill in the fridge for one hour.

While the dough chills, thinly slice the peaches and toss them with the sugar, cornstarch, and cinnamon.

Once the dough has chilled, transfer it to a lightly floured work surface.

Preheat the oven to 200°C (390°F).

Roll out the dough to 3 mm (⅛ in) thickness with a rolling pin. Roughly cut the dough into a fish shape, using a knife. Arrange the peach slices on the dough, starting at the tail and slightly overlapping each slice to create a fish scale pattern, leaving around a 3 cm/1¼ in border.

Fold the edges in and press them to seal in a fish shape. Add a chocolate chip for the eye, and add details to the fish tail with a knife. Mix the egg and water and brush the edges with egg wash.

Dot the filling with butter.

Bake for 30–35 minutes until the crust is golden brown.

Little Fish Pizzas

Fish-shaped pizza bianca, topped with thinly sliced zucchini and potato scales, makes for good summer snacks. Pack these miniatures for a seaside picnic or enjoy them as a refreshing poolside treat.

— MAKES 4 MINI PIZZAS —

1 batch of pizza dough
  (see recipe p. 31) or use
  store-bought pizza dough
  (around 250 g)

60 g (¼ cup) ricotta
25 g (¼ cup) grated Parmigiano
  Reggiano
35 g mozzarella
A pinch of salt and pepper to taste

2 small potatoes
½ zucchini
Fresh rosemary
Extra-virgin olive oil
Black olives
Red pepper flakes (optional)

TOOLS

Fish-shaped cookie cutter
  or a sharp knife
Paper straw cut to 1 cm (½ in)
Toothpick

If you are preparing the pizza dough yourself, see the base recipe on p. 31 for instructions. Roll out the dough to your desired thickness. If you are using store-bought dough, take it out of the fridge 15 minutes before preparation. Unpack the dough and unroll it.

Preheat the oven to 200°C (390°F).

Combine the ricotta, mozzarella, and Parmigiano Reggiano in a bowl with a pinch of salt and pepper to make the cheese mixture.

Thinly slice the potatoes and zucchini.

Cut the pizza dough into fish shapes using a knife or a cookie cutter. Cover the dough with the cheese mixture, then top with the sliced zucchini (sprinkled with red pepper flakes, if desired) and sliced potatoes (topped with rosemary sprigs).

Cut the black olives into eyes, using the paper straw as a cutter and the toothpick to push them out. Place the eyes on the fish and drizzle with olive oil.

Bake for 12–15 minutes, until the cheese mixture has melted and the crust is golden brown.

Chocolate Fish Twists

Puff pastry layered with chocolate spread is shaped and twisted
to resemble a fish. Enjoy eating your fish twist by twist.

 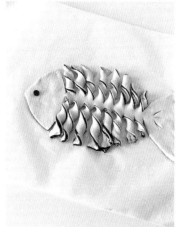

— MAKES 1 PUFF PASTY FISH —

1 store-bought, rectangular
package of puff pastry
100 g (⅓ cup) Nutella or
chocolate spread
1 chocolate chip

FOR THE EGG WASH
1 egg, whisked
1 tablespoon water

FOR THE CINNAMON SUGAR (OPTIONAL)
1 tablespoon sugar
1 teaspoon ground cinnamon

Preheat the oven to 200°C (390°F).

Unroll the puff pastry and spread it
thinly with Nutella. Fold the puff pastry in half so the shorter sides meet.
Using a knife, cut the pastry into a
fish shape. Add a chocolate chip for
the eye.

Make parallel cuts along both sides of
the body of the fish (see photo). Place
a chopstick in the middle of the fish
as a guideline, if needed.

Lift the strips one by one and twist
each twice (see photo).

For the egg wash, whisk the egg
and water together and brush the
fish with it.

Bake for about 15 minutes, until
golden brown.

If desired, mix the cinnamon and
sugar, sprinkle over the fish and serve.

Sfogliatine Glassate (Glazed Fish Cookies)

Sfogliatine glassate, meaning glazed puff pastry, are light and crunchy Italian cookies, glazed with icing sugar and apricot jam. Their usual diamond pattern reminded me of fish scales, so I've made them into fish shapes, drawing different "fish-scale" patterns with the jam. These fish will be a good companion for a leisurely coffee or tea break.

MAKES 8

1 store-bought, rectangular package of puff pastry

100 g (¾ cup) powdered sugar
1 egg white
50 g (2½ teaspoons) strawberry or apricot jam
Chocolate sprinkles

TOOLS
Fish-shaped cookie cutters (10 cm/4 in) or a sharp knife
Piping bag with a small round nozzle

Preheat the oven to 200°C (390°F).

Unroll the puff pastry and cut into 8 fish shapes using a fish cookie cutter or a knife.

Sift the powdered sugar into a bowl. Add the egg white and whisk until well combined. Evenly spread the egg white mixture onto each puff-pastry fish with a spatula or a brush.

Transfer the jam into a piping bag fitted with a small round nozzle and pipe diagonal stripes on each fish. Use chocolate sprinkles to create the eyes.

Bake for 15–20 minutes until golden brown. Let the cookies cool and serve.

Goldfish Cheese Crackers

Homemade goldfish cheese crackers are fashioned from white and orange cheeses that alternate in a stripe pattern, accented with thin nori strips. Serve these fish for summer snacks or add them to a cheeseboard, arranging them with Tête-de-Moine "coral" cheese and Parmesan tuiles to create an underwater cheese world.

MAKES 80–100

FOR THE CHEDDAR DOUGH
100 g (1 cup) orange cheddar, grated
100 g (¾ cup) all-purpose flour
50 g (3½ tablespoons) cold butter, cubed
3–4 tablespoons cold water

FOR THE GRUYÈRE DOUGH
100 g (½ cup) Gruyère or white cheddar, grated
100 g (¾ cup) all-purpose flour
50 g (3½ tablespoons) cold butter, cubed
3–4 tablespoons cold water

FOR THE DECORATION
Black sesame seeds
Nori seaweed sheets

TOOL
Fish-shaped cookie cutter or a sharp knife

FOR THE PARMESAN TUILE (OPTIONAL)
Approximately 100g (1 cup) Parmigiano Reggiano, grated

Preheat the oven to 175°C (350°F).

In a food processor, pulse the orange cheddar, flour, and butter until crumbly. Add the water one tablespoon at a time until the mixture comes together as a dough. On a flat surface, pat the dough into a disk shape and chill in the fridge for 1 hour.

Repeat the process for the Gruyère dough.

On a lightly floured work surface, roll each dough with a rolling pin into a 3 mm (⅛ in) thick rectangle. Cut the entire surface of the orange cheddar dough into thin strips for the fish stripes. Place the cheddar strips onto the Gruyère dough, making a yellow and orange striped pattern. Then lightly roll the dough again to press down the orange stripes.

Cut out the dough into fish shapes with a knife or a fish-shaped cookie cutter. Add black sesame seeds as eyes. Optionally, cut nori into thin strips and add as stripes to the fish cookies.

Bake for about 12–13 minutes.

To make the Parmesan tuile (optional), preheat the oven to 200°C (390°F).

On a baking sheet lined with parchment paper, sprinkle the Parmigiano Reggiano in the shape and size that you want to create coral reefs.

Bake for 3–5 minutes. Allow to cool, then carefully remove from the parchment paper and use as edible decor.

Place the goldfish in a scene with the Parmesan tuile or serve on their own.

Seashell

I love seashells and I search for them every time I visit a beach. Collecting seashells is like a treasure hunt. Each is unique, with an endless variety of shapes, sizes, colors, and patterns, which makes it impossible to say, "Oh, I already have the exact same one!" I believe people around the world can relate to the joy of discovering these natural gems.

Our love affair with seashells dates back to prehistoric times. Anthropologists have discovered 150,000-year-old remains of shell jewelry. In the 18th century, Europeans developed an obsession with seashells, leading them to become more valuable than the finest Baroque paintings. The folly was dubbed conchylomania, from the Latin *conchylium* (shell) and the Greek *mania* (madness). The reach of shells extended to numerous aspects of life, including currency, decoration, and art. The French rococo movement, for example, takes its name from the French word *rocaille*, meaning rock and shellwork. This fascination with seashells inspired countless artists and designers and continues to do so.

For me, seashells evoke happy memories of beach outings—walking barefoot on the sand, collecting shells, building sandcastles, and then decorating these palaces with newfound treasures. Others use them to create necklaces or bring them back home to display on shelves or tables. While the details may differ, the sentiment is universal: we all long to hold onto a piece of the beauty, joy, and serenity we experience around these precious souvenirs of summer.

Shell we have tea?

Teatime offers a pause in our day, a moment to breathe, and savor the simple pleasures.

Just as in *In Search of Lost Time* a taste of madeleines and tea takes Marcel Proust's character back through time, perhaps a cup of tea with one of these shell-shaped pastries will transport you back to your favorite summer memories, a short and sweet time travel for your teatime.

I hope these seashell treats infuse your teatime with similar emotions, reminding you of beach adventures, the sun's blissful warmth on your skin, salty sea breezes, and the carefree joy of collecting seashells—all while adding a touch of sweetness to your day.

So, "shell" we have tea?

Chocolate Conch-shaped Bread & Concha Cookie Bread

These are recipes for chocolate conch-shaped brioches filled with chocolate custard cream and for Japanese *melon pan,* which you could also call Mexican *conchas* (essentially a brioche bun covered in crunchy cookie dough to look like a seashell). I had known the latter bread as *melon pan* until I shared it on my Instagram and one of my followers told me that the Mexican *concha* is very similar, and that the word means "shell bread." I was thrilled to discover this shell (bread) connection, much like stumbling upon a new seashell on a sandy shore.

RECIPE ON THE NEXT PAGE

FOR THE BRIOCHE
(for both breads)
100 ml (scant ½ cup) lukewarm water
20 g (⅛ cup) sugar
1 teaspoon dried yeast
200 g (1½ cups) all-purpose flour
1 teaspoon salt
25 g egg (half of a large egg,
    yolk and white mixed)
25 g (scant 2 tablespoons) butter,
    softened

FOR THE COOKIE TOPPING
(for shell-shaped melon pan/concha)
25 g (scant 2 tablespoons) butter,
    softened
35 g (⅓ cup) sugar
25 g egg (rest of the egg above)
¼ teaspoon vanilla extract
75 g (½ cup) all-purpose flour

FOR THE CUSTARD CREAM
(for chocolate conch-shaped bread)
2 egg yolks
50 g (¼ cup) sugar
20 g (2½ tablespoons) all-purpose
    flour
200 ml (generous ¾ cup) milk
60 g (2 ounces) dark chocolate
    (65%–70%), coarsely chopped

FOR THE EGG WASH
1 egg
1 tablespoon water

TOOLS
Metal baking cones
    (12 cm/4.7 in or 14 cm/5.5 in)
Piping bag

BRIOCHE DOUGH
To make the brioche dough, place the lukewarm water, 1 teaspoon of sugar, and dried yeast in a small bowl and mix well. Allow the mixture to rest for 5–10 minutes until it bubbles up and becomes frothy.

In a large mixing bowl, combine the flour, salt, and the rest of the sugar. Pour in the yeast mixture along with the egg, and stir until a dough starts to form. Add the softened butter to the dough and knead until it becomes smooth and elastic, about 10 minutes.

Shape the dough into a ball and place it in a bowl. Cover the bowl with plastic wrap or a damp cloth and let it rise in a warm place for 1 hour, or until it has doubled in size.

Once it has risen, divide the brioche dough into 8 equal portions, shaping each into a smooth ball.

COOKIE TOPPING
To make the cookie topping, cream the softened butter and sugar together in a mixing bowl, followed by the egg and vanilla extract. Mix until well combined. Add the flour to the wet ingredients, mixing until a smooth cookie dough forms. Form a flat disk, wrap it with plastic wrap, and keep it in the fridge until ready to use.

CUSTARD CREAM
To make the chocolate custard cream, in a medium-sized heatproof (glass or metal) bowl, whisk together the egg yolks and sugar until they become light and creamy. Sift in the flour and mix well until you have a smooth paste.

Heat the milk in a saucepan over medium heat until it's just about to boil. Gradually add the warm milk to the egg mixture and continue whisking to make sure that the egg does not set.

Once fully combined, return the mixture to the saucepan. Cook over low heat, stirring continuously until thickened, so that a finger run over the back of a spoon leaves a mark.

Remove the pan from the heat and add the chocolate. Stir until the chocolate is completely melted and the custard is smooth.

Transfer the custard to a bowl and let it cool a little. Cover the bowl with plastic wrap, making sure the film touches the surface of the custard to prevent a skin from forming. Refrigerate for at least 1 hour.

CHOCOLATE CONCHES

To shape the chocolate conches (use 4 of the 8 brioche balls), roll out each dough ball into a long rope, about 1 cm (¼ in) diameter and 40 cm (15 in) length. Lightly grease the outside of 4 metal cones. Then, starting from the top of a metal cone, wrap 1 dough rope around it in a spiral. Repeat for the other 3.

Place the wrapped cones, seam side down, on a baking sheet lined with parchment paper, allowing enough space between them for expansion. Cover the baking sheet with plastic wrap or a damp cloth and let the dough rise 1.5 times in size, about 40 minutes.

Preheat the oven 190°C (375°F).

Brush the dough with egg wash. Bake for 12–13 minutes until golden brown

Remove the conches from the oven and let them cool on a wire rack for a few minutes before carefully removing the metal cones.

To assemble the chocolate conch-shaped bread, once the bread is completely cooled, using a piping bag, pipe the chocolate custard cream into each brioche conch. Serve immediately.

MELON PAN

For the melon pan/concha, use the remaining 4 brioche balls.

Divide the cookie dough into 4 equal portions. Roll out each portion between two sheets of plastic wrap or parchment paper, forming thin rounds that are slightly larger than the unbaked, risen brioche dough balls.

Place one cookie dough round on top of each brioche dough ball, gently pressing the edges to cover the top and sides of the brioche ball. Use a sharp knife or a dough scraper to create the lines of a shell in the cookie dough topping.

Place the brioches on a baking sheet lined with parchment paper, allowing enough space between them for expansion. Cover the baking sheet with plastic wrap or a damp cloth and let them rise again at room temperature for another 40 minutes, until 1.5 times their size.

Preheat the oven to 180°C (350°F).

Bake for 15 minutes, or until the tops are golden brown. Remove the bread from the oven and let it cool on a wire rack before serving.

Madeleines with a Chocolate Shell

These teatime classics and symbols of nostalgia were described by Marcel Proust as little cakes molded to look like the scalloped edges of a pilgrim's shell. Here, these shell-shaped cakes are coated in chocolate shells, for a shell under a shell.

— MAKES 12 —

100 g (¾ cup) all-purpose flour
A pinch of salt
½ teaspoon baking powder
2 eggs (100 g), room temperature
100 g (½ cup) sugar
1 teaspoon vanilla extract
100 g (7 tablespoons) butter, melted
150 g (5.5 ounces) coating chocolate (white, milk, dark, according to your preference)

TOOLS
Madeleine mold (metal or silicon, though silicon is easier if including the chocolate coating)
Kitchen thermometer

Note: The general rule for madeleines is a 1:1:1:1 ratio of eggs, flour, butter, and sugar. So start by measuring the weight of your eggs and then adjust the rest of the ingredients' weight accordingly. I am using measurements assuming 2 eggs weigh 100 g (3.5 ounces).

I recommend using "coating" chocolate or candy melts (for various colors) to ensure that the chocolate coating slips easily from the mold when using a metal pan. If you are using couverture chocolate, make sure it is tempered very well.

In a medium-sized mixing bowl, whisk together the flour, salt, and baking powder. Set aside.

In a separate large mixing bowl, using an electric mixer, whisk together the eggs and sugar until pale and frothy. Gradually fold the dry ingredients into the wet ingredients, mixing until just combined. Be careful not to overmix the batter. Gently add the vanilla extract and the slightly cooled melted butter (around 45°C/115°F) into the batter, and mix well until the butter is completely incorporated. Cover the batter with plastic wrap and let it rest in the refrigerator for 30 minutes to 1 hour.

Preheat the oven to 180°C (350°F).

After the batter has rested, spoon or pipe it into the generously buttered and floured madeleine pan, filling each mold about ¾ full.

Bake for 10–12 minutes, or until the edges are golden brown and the centers spring back when lightly touched.

Remove the madeleines from the oven and let them cool in the pan for a few minutes before transferring them to a wire rack to cool completely.

To make the coating, melt the chocolate in a bowl over a saucepan full of simmering water. Spoon about 1 tablespoon of melted chocolate into each madeleine mold.

Lightly press the cooled madeleines into the chocolate, ensuring they align well with the mold. Then place the mold into the refrigerator or freezer and let it chill for 10–20 minutes.

Once set, remove the chocolate-coated madeleines from the mold and serve.

Shell S'mores Tarts

Graham cracker crusts are filled with dark chocolate ganache and
topped with toasted meringue piped into the ridged shape of a shell,
combining two beach favorites: seashells and a bonfire.

MAKES 5 MINI TARTS (10 CM/4 IN)

FOR THE CRUST
240 g graham crackers (about 16)
Or
215 g digestive biscuits (14 biscuits)
120 g (8 tablespoons) butter, melted
20 g (⅛ cup packed) brown sugar
¼ teaspoon cinnamon

FOR THE GANACHE
400 g (14 ounces) dark chocolate
    (60%–75%), coarsely chopped
250 ml (1 cup) heavy cream
50 g (3½ tablespoons) butter
½ teaspoon salt

FOR THE MERINGUE
4 large egg whites
200 g (1 cup) sugar

TOOLS
5 mini tart pans (10 cm/4 in)
    with removable bottoms
Piping bag
Kitchen torch
Kitchen thermometer

To make the crust, in a food processor, pulse the graham crackers or digestive biscuits until they become fine crumbs.

Add the melted butter (and brown sugar and cinnamon if using digestive biscuits). Pulse until the mixture is well combined and resembles wet sand. Press the mixture into the bottom and up the sides of 5 mini tart pans. Chill the crust in the refrigerator for at least 30 minutes to set.

To make the chocolate ganache filling, combine the dark chocolate, heavy cream, butter, and salt in a heatproof (metal or glass) bowl. Heat the mixture over a saucepan full of simmering water until the chocolate is melted and the mixture is smooth.

Pour the chocolate ganache into the chilled tart crusts, spreading it evenly with a spatula. Refrigerate the tarts for at least 2 hours, or until the ganache is set.

To make the meringue topping, combine the egg whites and sugar in a heatproof (metal or glass) bowl. Place the bowl over a saucepan of simmering water, ensuring that the bottom of the bowl does not touch the water. Whisk the egg white mixture continuously until the sugar is completely dissolved and the mixture reaches a temperature of 70°C (160°F). Remove the bowl from the heat and transfer the warm egg-white mixture to a large bowl.

Using a stand or hand mixer, beat the egg-white mixture on medium-high speed until stiff peaks form.

To assemble, remove the tarts from the refrigerator once the chocolate ganache is set. Using a piping bag with a decorative tip (round or star), pipe the meringue onto the tarts in seashell shapes.

Use a kitchen torch to lightly brown the meringue, creating a toasted appearance.

Optional: Serve with pearl chocolates on a bed of biscuits crumbled to look like sand.

Seashell Macarons

Seashell-shaped macarons with a white chocolate ganache
and pearl chocolate inside are dainty and precious, like the little
shells we pick up on the shore.

FOR THE MACARON SHELLS
80 g (generous ¾ cup) almond flour
80 g (½ cup) powdered sugar
2 egg whites (65 g), room temperature
65 g (½ cup) granulated sugar
1 teaspoon of cocoa powder

FOR THE FILLING
160 g (5½ ounces) white chocolate,
   coarsely chopped
100 ml (⅓ cup) heavy cream
A pinch of salt

FOR THE DECORATION
White pearl chocolates

TOOLS
2 piping bags

To make the macaron shells, sift together the almond flour and powdered sugar in a bowl.

In a separate bowl, whip the egg whites with an electric mixer on medium speed until frothy. Gradually add the granulated sugar while continuously beating the mixture. Once all the sugar has been added, whip until very stiff, glossy peaks form.

Slowly fold the sifted dry ingredients into the meringue with a spatula until fully incorporated.

Split the batter into two equal halves. Stir the cocoa powder into one half. Carefully blend each half of the batter until it becomes smooth and shiny (*macaronage*). The batter should slowly flow off the spatula when lifted.

Fill a piping bag with both batters, adding them from opposite sides, so that both the vanilla and chocolate batter are dispensed simultaneously when piped.

Pipe the batter onto a baking sheet lined with a Teflon sheet or two baking papers, following the shapes on a macaron template (either round or shell-shaped) or piping them into shell shapes freehand.

After piping, tap the baking sheet on the counter several times to remove any air bubbles. Use a toothpick to pop bubbles if needed.

Allow the piped macarons to rest at room temperature for about 30 minutes or until their surfaces are dry to the touch.

Preheat the oven to 150°C (300°F).

Bake the macarons for about 15 minutes. Let them cool completely before removing them from the baking sheet.

To make the filling, place the white chocolate in a heat-proof bowl.

In a small saucepan, heat the heavy cream until it begins to simmer. Pour the simmering cream over the chopped white chocolate and gently stir the mixture until it becomes smooth.

Let the ganache cool to room temperature, then chill in the fridge for about 1 hour or until thickened to peanut butter consistency.

Using a whisk, whip the ganache until slightly fluffy and pale in color, ensuring not to over-whip.

To assemble, transfer the whipped ganache to a piping bag, then pipe it onto the macaron shells. Place a pearl chocolate in the center and sandwich with another shell.

Place the macarons in an airtight container and chill in the fridge for at least 1 hour before serving.

Tiramisu in a Shell

This is a tiramisu in a shell-shaped dish, which conceals layers of espresso-soaked ladyfingers and mascarpone cream under a cocoa-dusted shell.

MAKES 3 SHELLS (SERVES 6)

3 egg yolks
4 tablespoons granulated sugar
½ teaspoon vanilla extract
225 g (¾ cup) mascarpone
180 ml (¾ cup) heavy cream
100 g (3.5 ounces) ladyfingers
125 ml (½ cup) espresso,
  cooled to room temperature
Cocoa powder

OPTIONAL
1 tablespoon of alcohol of your
  choice (kahlua, marsala, rum,
  amaretto, etc.)

TOOLS
Seashell-shaped dishes
Kitchen thermometer
Piping bag

In a heatproof (metal or glass) bowl, combine the egg yolks, 2 tablespoons sugar, and vanilla extract. Place the bowl over a saucepan of simmering water, ensuring the bottom of the bowl does not touch the water. Whisk the mixture continuously until it's pale and creamy and reaches 70°C (160°F). Remove the bowl from the heat and let the mixture cool slightly. Add the mascarpone to the egg mixture and mix until well combined.

In a separate bowl, using an electric mixer, whisk the heavy cream and the remaining 2 tablespoons of sugar until stiff peaks form. Gently fold the whipped cream into the mascarpone mixture until well combined.

Spread a thin layer of the resulting mascarpone cream into a shell-shaped dish. Quickly dip both sides of the ladyfinger biscuits into the espresso (mixed with alcohol, optional), and arrange them over the mascarpone cream in the shell-shaped dish. Top the ladyfingers with another thin layer of the mascarpone cream.

Finish by piping the remaining mascarpone cream over the ladyfingers, following the seashell lines or patterns on the dish. Refrigerate for several hours to allow the tiramisu to set.

Before serving, dust with cocoa powder.

Leaf

Autumn is when leaves become the stars of the show. In spring, flowers claim our attention. In summer, we are blinded by the sun, and the blue sky and lush green trees form a continuous blur, like an impressionistic landscape.

Finally in autumn, leaves start changing colors and falling from the trees, and we actually notice their individual character. Yellow ginkgo, red maple, orange oak— all shapes, colors, and sizes contribute to the majestic autumn foliage, which is a feast for the eyes.

As the season advances and more leaves
fall and pile up on the ground, the autumn
symphony is amplified by the sounds of
footsteps on crunchy leaves, their rustle in the
evening breeze, and the crackling of a campfire.
Each recipe in this chapter is inspired by
my favorite autumn activities: viewing the
autumn foliage, catching falling leaves,
collecting leaves and pressing them inside a
book, stepping on piles of crunchy leaves, and
making campfires and s'mores.

Apple Leaves
Vin Chaud

Apples, with their colors ranging from light green to dark red, remind me of autumn foliage. I love that my two favorites of the season—apples and leaves—resemble each other.

Danpung nori (단풍놀이) is a Korean compound word that I adore, too. *Danpung* means tinted autumn leaves and *nori* means play or entertainment. *Danpung nori* together, therefore, means "autumn foliage play." It refers to a traditional Korean autumn activity of heading outdoors to view autumn foliage, to entertain oneself with the beauty of nature and engage in activities including picnics, walks, hikes, or restful moments on benches in view of dazzling colors. Similarly, in Japan, there is *momijigari* (meaning "autumn leaves hunting"). People visit iconic autumn foliage havens—temples, parks, mountains—to admire trees dressed in warm hues.

So in autumn, I would often invite or be invited by friends and family for *danpung nori* or *momijigari*. We would feel as if we had stepped into a warm toned painting, sipping cozy drinks of our choice: apple cider, hot wine, or sake. Apple "leaves" vin chaud is *danpung nori* in a cup, a sip of autumn—a perfect way to appreciate the beauty of autumn leaves and quite literally drink it in, too.

MAKES 6–8 SERVINGS

3 apples (1 sliced and cored, 2 for decoration)
750 ml (3 cups) white wine
250 ml (1 cup) apple juice
75 g (¾ cup) sugar
2 cinnamon sticks
1 star anise pod
3 cloves
1 orange (½ zested, the rest to slice and serve as decoration)

TOOLS
Leaf-shaped cookie cutters or a sharp knife
Sieve

Note: For a non-alcoholic version, replace the wine with the same volume of apple juice and do not add the sugar.

Cut leaf shapes out of the apples by pressing cookie cutters 4 cm (1½ in) deep into the surface and then gently lifting and pressing them out. Carve the details of leaf veins with a paring knife.

In a large pot, combine all the ingredients (except the apples and oranges used for decoration) and bring to a simmer until the sugar is dissolved.

Turn off the heat and let the wine infuse for 15–20 minutes. Then strain through a fine-mesh sieve.

Pour the wine into teacups. Serve each steaming cup with a slice of orange and leaf-shaped apple pieces. You can also add a cinnamon stick and star anise to each cup (optional).

Autumn Colors Fruit Leather

As a child, I used to collect colorful leaves of different shapes and sizes in autumn. I would bring them home and press them between the pages of heavy books. There was satisfaction in taking the leaves out a few days later to find them flattened and dried so neatly.

At times, I would forget where I had stashed them. Discovering pressed leaves in a book months or even a year later felt like receiving a love letter from autumn. It left me surprised but warm and fuzzy inside. With these flat, colorful, and delicious "leaves," you can give love letters, too.

──────────── MAKES 30–40 LEAVES ────────────

200 g raspberries
3–4 apricots, pitted and diced
1–2 mangoes, pitted, peeled and cubed
10 g (2½ ounces) baby spinach
2 apples, peeled and cored
Sugar (optional if fruit is not sweet enough)
Lemon juice

TOOL
Leaf-shaped cookie cutter or a sharp knife

Note: You can use fresh or frozen fruit.

To make the raspberry puree, pulse the raspberries in a blender until smooth. Transfer the puree to a saucepan and cook with 3 tablespoons of sugar for about 10 minutes until thick and jammy.

For the apricot puree, pulse the apricots in a blender with 1 teaspoon lemon juice and 1–2 tablespoons water until smooth. Transfer the puree to a saucepan and cook for about 10 minutes until thick and jammy.

For the mango puree, pulse the mangoes in a blender until smooth. Transfer the puree to a saucepan and cook for about 10 minutes until thick and jammy.

For the apple-spinach puree, pulse the apples in a blender with 1 teaspoon of lemon juice and 1–2 tablespoons of water until smooth. Transfer the puree to a saucepan and cook for about 10 minutes until thick and jammy. Let the apple mixture cool and transfer back to the blender. Add spinach and blend together.

Place a silicon mat or parchment paper on a rimmed baking sheet. Pour the purees onto the lined baking sheet from left to right, one next to the other, in this order: raspberry (red), apricot (orange), mango (yellow), apple-spinach (green). Bake at 100°C (212°F) for 2–3 hours (depending on the thickness) until it's dry.

Cool thoroughly, then cut the fruit roll-ups into leaf shapes using cookie cutters.

Falling Leaf Cinnamon Twists

After the ravishingly gorgeous days of *danpung nori*, or *momijigari*, or, in English, leaf peeping, leaves start falling slowly from the trees.

There is a belief in Korea that if you are able to catch a falling leaf, it will bring you good fortune. Perhaps because of this myth, ever since I was a kid, whenever I walk by or stand under trees with falling leaves, I try to catch one, hoping that it will bring me good luck.

Catching a falling leaf is not as easy as it may sound. There was, however, one special autumn day. I was sitting on a bench under a tree, reading. Leaves were falling from the tree, and one landed perfectly on the page so I could catch it. I still remember how exhilarated I felt, the joy and excitement such a falling leaf brought me that day. I remained happy for the rest of the day, wondering if something nice would happen to me—and if so, what would it be? I don't remember if something extraordinary happened, or if that leaf really had the magic power to bring good luck. But maybe the magic is in how happy that little falling leaf made me one autumn day. Enough that I am still always excited to catch the next one.

— MAKES 12 —

1 store-bought, rectangular package of puff pastry
25 g (2 tablespoons) butter, melted
50 g (½ cup) brown sugar
1 teaspoon ground cinnamon

1 egg, whisked
1 tablespoon water

Preheat the oven to 200°C (390°F).

Unroll the puff pastry and brush it with melted butter.

In a small bowl, mix the brown sugar and ground cinnamon. Sprinkle the cinnamon sugar over the puff pastry, then fold the dough in half so the shorter sides meet.

Cut the puff pastry into ovals with a knife. Make 3 vertical slits in the middle of the dough (don't cut the ends of the dough). Push one end of the oval through the middle slit and gently press the dough through to create a ribbon shape.

Mix the egg and water and brush each leaf with egg wash.

Bake for 15 minutes until golden brown.

STEP 1

STEP 2

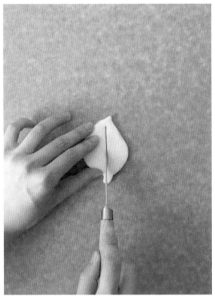

STEP 3

STEP 7

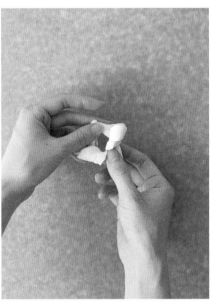

STEP 8

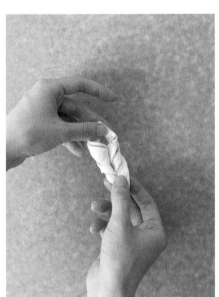

STEP 9

STEP 4

STEP 5

STEP 6

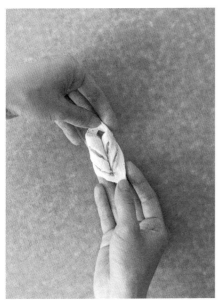

STEP 10

STEP 11

STEP 12

"Crunchy Leaves" Apple Pie

When fallen leaves pile up, like caramel-colored carpets laid out on gardens and walkways, the autumn experience shifts from visual to auditory. The satisfying and addictive game of stepping on crispy dried leaves: I loved it when I was a kid and I still love it today, as do many of my family and friends. I find it to be universal: no matter what age you are, or where you are from, you will most likely take pleasure in the simple act that transports you to carefree childhood, when you lived in the moment and purely relished the season without thinking.

This double-crust apple pie covered in pie-crust leaves will remind you of all the blankets of autumn leaves that have ever tempted you to jump in or stomp on them. Cutting each slice will recreate the sound of autumn that made you—and still makes you—happy.

— MAKES 1 PIE —

FOR THE DOUGH
400 g (3 cups) all-purpose flour
250 g (1 cup) cold butter, cubed
4 tablespoons sugar
1 teaspoon salt
6 tablespoons ice water

FOR THE FILLING
5–6 apples, peeled and cored
120 g (½ cup) sugar
2 tablespoons cornstarch
½ teaspoon ground cinnamon
2 teaspoons (10 g) butter,
   cut into small cubes

FOR THE EGG WASH
1 egg
1 tablespoon water

TOOLS
Tart tin or pie dish (30 cm/12 in)
   with a removable bottom
Leaf-shaped cookie cutters or
   a sharp knife

In a food processor, pulse the flour, butter, sugar, and salt until crumbly. Add ice water one tablespoon at a time until the mixture comes together as a dough. Divide the dough in half, form two round disks, wrap in plastic wrap, and chill in the fridge for 1 hour.

Preheat the oven to 200°C (390°F).

To make the filling, thinly slice the apples and toss with sugar, cinnamon, and cornstarch.

On a lightly floured work surface, roll out one portion of dough with a rolling pin into a 35 cm (14 in) diameter circle and transfer to a greased pie dish. Press the dough against the sides and bottom of the pie dish. Roll out the second portion of dough and cut it into small leaves using cookie cutters.

Spoon the apple mixture into the pie dish and dot with butter. Then arrange the leaf cut-outs on top, leaving some openings as vents, so the hot steam from inside the pie can escape.

Mix the egg and water and brush the top with egg wash.

Place the pie on the lower rack of the oven. Bake for 20 minutes, then reduce the temperature to 180°C (355°F) and bake for about 1 hour until the pie is golden brown.

Note: If you have extra cut-out leaves after covering the pie, brush them with the egg wash and bake them separately at 180°C (355°F) for 10 minutes until golden brown. You can add them to the pie before serving for the extra effect of a leaf pile and extra crunch!

Leaf-shaped Biscuits for S'mores

Camping holds a special place in my family's hearts as a long-treasured tradition. Ever since I can remember, we went camping every season, and we still do today. Each season has its own charm, but my personal favorite is autumn camping. A spectrum of warm hues against a clear blue sky, leaves shimmering golden in autumn sunlight, and crisp, chill air combined with shorter days and longer evenings just calls for cozy campfires.

The best part of camping for me, especially as a kid, was the campfire and s'mores. We would gather around the glow, telling stories, listening to music, singing along, and roasting marshmallows. Being allowed to play with fire, getting a sugar rush from a s'mores sandwich, and being able to stay up late made me covet these fun, adventurous childhood times. Today, a campfire is relaxing. There is something soothing about its warmth and the colorful movement of flames. The crackling calms and comforts me, melting away the worries or concerns I might have as an adult. But I still have the same excitement for the s'mores. Toasted marshmallow—soft and gooey inside—with dark chocolate slightly melted from the heat, sandwiched between warm-spiced biscuits shaped like crunchy leaves ... these never fail to bring me the same warm and cozy feeling as autumn's evening campfires, whether enjoyed at home or outdoors.

RECIPE ON THE NEXT PAGE

MAKES 30 BISCUITS FOR 15 S'MORES

150 g (1⅛ cup) whole wheat flour
½ teaspoon ground cinnamon
½ teaspoon baking soda
½ teaspoon salt
50 g (¼ cup) light brown sugar
70 g (5 tablespoons) butter, softened
2 tablespoons milk
2 tablespoons honey
1 teaspoon vanilla extract

15 marshmallows
1–2 bars of good quality
   dark chocolate

TOOL
Leaf shaped cookie cutter or
   sharp knife

In a large bowl, mix the flour, cinnamon, baking soda, and salt.

In a separate bowl, using an electric mixer, cream the sugar and butter until fluffy (a few minutes). Gradually incorporate the flour mixture. Add the milk, honey, and vanilla extract and beat until the mixture forms a dough. Make a round disk, wrap in plastic wrap, and chill in the fridge for 1 hour.

Once chilled, transfer the dough to a lightly floured work surface.

Preheat the oven to 175°C (350°F).

Roll the dough to 3 mm (⅛ in) thickness and cut leaf shapes using a cookie cutter or a knife.

Bake for 10–12 minutes.

Toast the marshmallows until gooey over a campfire or in a frying pan. To assemble your s'mores, cradle the toasted marshmallows and dark chocolate squares between two leaf biscuits.

Mushroom

Mushrooms remind me of late autumn walks in the forest.

I like late autumn rambles as they offer a serene, soothing transition into winter. The ground that once felt like a crunchy carpet of golden leaves feels more like a padded cushion, having softened in the autumn rain. The earthy aroma of rain-soaked soil, the distinct musky scent of fallen leaves beginning to decompose, and the fresh scent of rain mingle. The light, too, changes. No longer direct and intense as in the summertime, and no longer bouncing off verdant greens, autumn light is softer: absorbed by the dark, wet forest, it is diffused, spreading its mellow, moody atmosphere, amplifying the sense of mystery.

In the midst of this tranquil woodland scene, mushrooms emerge as unexpected treasures. Mushrooms are magical and mysterious; perhaps that's why they figure in folklore and fairy tales, or as the magical mushrooms in Alice's Wonderland that change her size with a single bite. The term "fairy ring", a circle where mushrooms have sprung up, continues the fantastical narrative, as people believed it was created for fairies to dance and dwell.

Each encounter with a mushroom, diverse in shape, size, and color, brings a surge of joy and a sense of discovery, adding a touch of wonder to the stroll.

The silent forest, with its softened autumn light and enchanting mushrooms dotting the forest floor, it's a sight of great beauty tinged with a hint of melancholy, for it ushers in the close of another year.

Steamed "Mushroom" Buns with Sweet Red Beans

In Korea, the appearance of steamed buns in corner stores (convenience stores these days) is a sign that winter is just around the corner. Getting a hot steamed bun—with its filling of sweet red bean paste or savory vegetables or pork—has become a tradition marking the transition from autumn to winter. With these buns in my hand, I feel ready for winter, as though I am putting on a snug pair of gloves or a cozy scarf, giving me the confidence that I will survive the long and cold days ahead.

———————————————— MAKES 6 ————————————————

1 tablespoon sugar
½ teaspoon yeast
80 ml (⅓ cup) lukewarm water
150 g (1 cup) all-purpose flour
A pinch of salt
½ teaspoon baking powder
1 tablespoon neutral oil

1 tablespoon cocoa powder
1 tablespoon water

120 g (½ cup) sweetened red
    bean paste for the filling

TOOL
Bamboo (or metal) steamer basket

In a small bowl, combine ½ teaspoon of sugar, yeast, and lukewarm water. Allow the mixture to sit for about 5–10 minutes until it bubbles up and becomes frothy.

In a medium bowl, mix the flour, salt, baking powder and the rest of the sugar. Add the yeast mixture to the dry ingredients and knead until they form a smooth dough. Add the oil and knead another 10 minutes, until the dough is soft. Cover the dough and let it rise until it doubles in size, approximately 1 hour.

Divide the red bean paste into 6 portions, about 20 g (1½ table-spoons) each, and shape each into a soft ball.

Once the dough has doubled in size, divide it into 6 portions, each weighing around 40 g (1½ ounces).

Reserve a small portion of each dough piece, around 5–7 g (or ⅛ of the dough piece), and shape it into a short stick to resemble a mushroom stem. Repeat.

Flatten the larger dough pieces (about 35 g each), place the red bean paste in the center, then gather and pinch the dough at the top to completely enclose the filling. Repeat this process with the rest of the dough. Flatten the dough balls on one side to resemble the caps of mushrooms.

In a small bowl, mix the cocoa powder and water, and brush the cocoa mixture onto the dome of each bun.

Cover the formed buns and let them rise for an additional 20 minutes.

Carefully place the buns into a steamer and steam for about 14 minutes. Add the dough stems and steam for another 1–2 minutes for a total of 16 minutes.

Once the buns have cooled slightly, create a small hole at the bottom of each bun, insert a dough stem, and serve while warm.

Choco-Mushrooms Chocolate Cookies

A playful nod to a beloved Korean snack from my childhood, these "choco-mushrooms" are chocolate "mushroom caps" on a cookie "stem." They came in a uniform shape, packed in a box, but I've taken the liberty of diverging from the traditional design, drawing inspiration from the diverse mushroom varieties I encounter during forest walks and the ones I pick up at farmers markets in autumn. So feel free to get creative: you can experiment with different colors of chocolate, create unique patterns on your mushroom caps, or vary the shapes of your cookie stems for a fun and quirky touch. Create an autumnal forest right on your table for your tea or coffee break.

— MAKES ABOUT 50 —

45 g (3 tablespoons) butter
3 tablespoons sugar
½ teaspoon vanilla extract
100 g (¾ cup) all-purpose flour
A pinch of salt
3 tablespoons milk

300 g (10½ ounces) chocolate of your
   choice (white, milk, or dark)

TOOL
Mushroom-, cone-, or semi-
   sphere-shaped chocolate mold

To make the cookie stems, preheat the oven to 170°C (340°F).

In a medium-sized bowl, cream the butter and sugar together until well combined. Stir in the vanilla extract. Incorporate the flour and salt into the butter mixture. Gradually add the milk, one tablespoon at a time, mixing until a dough forms.

Craft the dough into an assortment of mushroom stem shapes, varying the lengths and thickness for a realistic touch.

Bake on a parchment-lined baking sheet for roughly 15 minutes or until the edges are lightly browned.

To make the chocolate mushroom caps, place your chosen chocolate in a heat-resistant bowl and set over a pan of simmering water. Stir until the chocolate has melted.

Transfer the melted chocolate to a piping bag. Pipe the chocolate into your mold.

Once the chocolate has partially set but is still soft, insert the cookie stems into the middle of the mold, position-ing them so they stand up straight.

Allow your creations to cool in the fridge for 20–30 minutes, or until the chocolate has fully set and the mushrooms can easily be removed from the mold.

To serve, arrange your chocolate mushroom cookies on a bed of crushed Oreo or chocolate cookie crumbs for a "freshly foraged" look.

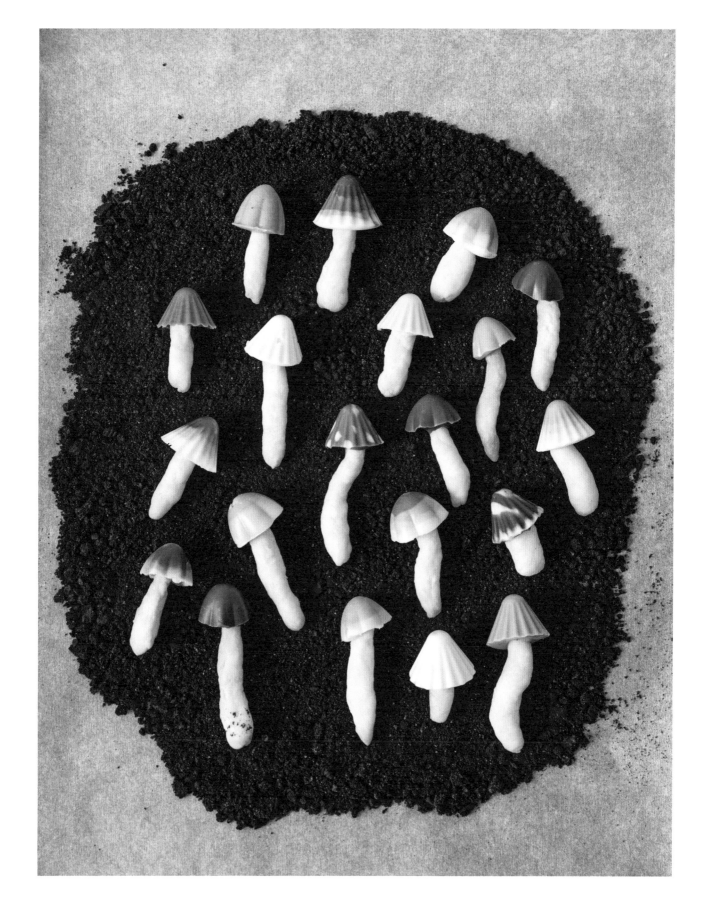

"Forest Mushroom" Meringues

Meringues that look like mushrooms can take on various shapes depending on how you pipe and color them. I like to serve them for dessert, with a dollop of whipped cream, dusted with Oreo cookie crumbs or matcha crumbles to mimic the look of a forest floor.

MAKES 35

FOR THE MERINGUE
2 egg whites
¼ teaspoon cream of tartar
A pinch of salt
100 g (½ cup) granulated sugar
½ teaspoon vanilla extract

Cocoa powder to dust
100 g (3½ ounces) chocolate
   to assemble

TOOL
Piping bag

To make the meringue, preheat the oven to 100°C (210°F).

Separate the egg whites from the yolks, ensuring no yolk gets into the whites.

Whip the egg whites and cream of tartar with a pinch of salt using a stand or hand mixer until frothy.

Gradually add the sugar, one spoonful at a time, while continuing to whip the egg whites. Once the mixture forms stiff, glossy peaks, add the vanilla extract. To test the meringue mixture, rub a small amount between your fingers—it should feel smooth, not grainy. If it's grainy, whip a bit longer.

Transfer the meringue to a piping bag fitted with a round nozzle.

Line a baking sheet with parchment paper. Pipe the meringue to create two shapes: the caps and the stems of the mushrooms. They will be assembled later.

Bake the meringues for about 1 hour or until they easily peel off the parchment paper. Turn off the oven and let the meringues cool completely inside for 1–2 hours.

Once they are cooled, melt the chocolate in a heat-resistant bowl over a pot of hot water and use the chocolate to "glue" the two parts of the mushrooms together, shaving the top of the stem to flatten it if needed.

Dust the meringue mushrooms with cocoa powder, rubbing them around for a darker color, if desired.

Serve the mushroom meringues with whipped cream dusted with Oreo crumbs (or chocolate cookie crumbs) or matcha crumble for a forest scenario.

Deconstructed "Forest Floor" Cake

Mushroom meringues also serve as elegant decorations for chocolate cakes, stacked to resemble a tree stump or roughly broken into pieces as deconstructed cake.

—— SERVES 6–8 (15 CM/6 IN) ——

FOR THE CHOCOLATE CAKE

120 g (1 cup) all-purpose flour
180 g (1 scant cup) sugar
30 g (¼ cup) cocoa powder
½ teaspoon baking powder
½ teaspoon baking soda
½ teaspoon salt
120 ml (½ cup) milk
60 ml (¼ cup) neutral vegetable oil
   (sunflower seed, grapeseed, etc.)
1 egg
1 teaspoon vanilla extract
100 ml (generous ⅓ cup) hot coffee

FOR THE VANILLA CREAM

300 ml (1¼ cups) heavy cream
3 tablespoons powdered sugar
½ teaspoon vanilla extract

Note: Since meringues can be quite sweet, this cream is made on the less sweet side. Feel free to adjust the level of sweetness according to your preference.

FOR THE MATCHA CRUMBLE

50 g (½ cup) almond flour
60 g (½ cup) all-purpose flour
1–2 teaspoons matcha powder
   (depending on your preference)
50 g (¼ cup) granulated sugar
50 g (3½ tablespoons) cold butter,
   cubed

CHOCOLATE CAKE

For the chocolate cake, preheat the oven to 175°C (350°F). Prepare three 15 cm (6 in) round cake pans by lining them with parchment paper.

In a large mixing bowl, combine the flour, sugar, cocoa powder, baking powder, baking soda, and salt.

In another bowl, whisk together the milk, oil, egg, and vanilla extract until they're well combined.

Gradually add the wet ingredients to the dry ingredients, mixing well until the batter is smooth.

Slowly pour in the hot coffee, stirring continuously. The batter will be thin.

Divide the batter equally among the prepared pans.

Bake for about 30 minutes, or until a toothpick inserted into the center of the cakes comes out clean.

Let the cakes cool in the pans for about 15 minutes, then remove them from the pans and transfer to a wire rack to cool completely.

VANILLA CREAM

For the vanilla cream, combine the heavy cream, powdered sugar, and vanilla extract in a medium-sized bowl. Whip the mixture with a hand or stand mixer until it reaches your desired consistency, forming either soft or stiff peaks depending on your preference.

MATCHA CRUMBLE

To make the matcha crumble, preheat the oven to 135°C (275°F).

In a medium-sized bowl, combine the almond flour, all-purpose flour, matcha powder, and granulated sugar. Stir until all the ingredients are well distributed.

Add the cold, cubed butter to the dry ingredients. Using your fingers or a pastry cutter, rub the butter into the mixture until it resembles coarse crumbs.

Spread the crumble mixture on a baking sheet lined with parchment paper. Try to spread it evenly to ensure uniform baking.

Bake for approximately 20 minutes. The goal is to dry out the crumble without browning it (to maintain the green color).

Remove from the oven and allow to cool. The crumble will become crisper as it cools.

Assemble and serve the cake as desired.

Closing

Yet it's in this closure that I find anticipation for another cycle of seasons and the adventures they hold, ready to unfold with the promise of a new year.

As the final hues of autumn fade, giving way to winter's crisp chill, the last leaves fall and the first snowflakes dance in the air. Life enters a phase of dormancy, drawing us into long, quiet, dark nights, gently reminding us of nature's cycles and the magic present in each stage.

In the coming year there will be more
beautiful moments to share and discover,
from the first bloom of spring to the last
mushroom dotting the forest floor.
Each season in nature gifts us with
its own unique treasures and
wonderful memories.

Until we meet again, may the beauty,
wonder, and joy of nature fill your life,
inspire you, and translate into exquisite
food art on your table.

Table-setting & Tool Guide

Setting the table
—indoors—

DECK YOUR TABLE WITH

– 1 –

Linen Tablecloths: I like that linen is forgiving—slight wrinkles can lend a rustic yet romantic appeal. Personally, I prefer oversize table-cloths that reach or even gently drape onto the floor, as this lends an air of romanticism to the setting.

– 2 –

Seasonal Accents: Incorporate items that reflect the season, such as flowers or fruits. You don't need an abundance of blooms; just a few, carefully placed in individual vases or even champagne flutes, can work wonders. Likewise, fruits thoughtfully arranged in a footed fruit bowl or casually scattered around the table can make an attractive centerpiece or decoration. For autumn, dry wheat brings harvest charm. In winter, when the table is not adorned in festive attire, elements such as evergreen tree branches or pine cones introduce a wintery atmosphere, reflecting the season's serenity and beauty.

– 3 –

Candles and candlesticks: I source my candlesticks and candelabra in numerous places, from modern design shops to vintage or antique stores. The variety of materials, from glass to silver and brass to ceramic conveys a unique mood. Ceramic brings a sense of warmth, ideal for colder months, while glass lends a cool touch to summery table settings. Consider long, elegant candles for that extra special touch (you can also coordinate their color with the table setting for a harmonious look).

Setting the table
—outdoors—

IN OUTDOOR DINING, SIMPLICITY IS KEY.

– 1 –

Start by selecting an ideal spot. If you have a breathtaking view,
you need little else.

– 2 –

Pack a simple feast, such as galettes and focaccia, which
are travel-friendly, perhaps accompanied by a bottle of wine.

– 3 –

Add a rustic tablecloth to your table or even spread it
directly on the grass or sand for a picnic.

– 4 –

Keep things relaxed. Full cutlery sets are unnecessary when
dining is made to be enjoyed with the hands.

– 5 –

Consider wooden tableware such as boards and plates
—for both their natural aesthetic and their practicality—
so you can feast without worrying about breakage.

Sea-salted air will enhance your meal's flavors, and the golden
hue of the setting sun will add warmth to your food. It's all about
embracing and appreciating the beauty of the natural setting.

Tools

Over the years, I've built up a collection of cookie cutters in diverse shapes and sizes. They have definitely helped with my creations, especially the smaller ones (around 1–2 cm), as such sizes can be intricate to cut out by hand. When I'm on the hunt for a specific shape, I find these tools in local baking shops, at vintage or antique stores, and even online.

While cookie cutters have greatly facilitated my work, using a knife or scissors to fashion shapes will bring personal, organic touches to your creations. It not only adds the authenticity of nature but also ensures that your dishes are truly one-of-a-kind, transcending the typical "cookie-cutter" approach. So please do not hesitate to take matters into your own hands!

Categories

Ingredients

Celine is a Korean-born food blogger and stylist now living
in Switzerland, celebrated on Instagram (@celineyrs) for her
creative and visually appealing food content. Drawing from her
experiences in Korea, Japan, France, and the U.S., she uniquely
combines cooking, styling, and photography to share her passion
for food storytelling.

First and foremost, I wish to express my sincere gratitude to the Prestel publishing team: Claudia, Veronika, Eve, Lena, and Luisa. Each one of you has breathed life into my vision. With your meticulous attention to details and thoughtful touches, you transformed it into the beautiful reality that these pages now hold.

Special thanks to my one and only, Antoine. Your encouragement nudged me to embark on this creative journey. Your contributions to my work have been invaluable, from sampling recipes to capturing charming images of little bees and helping me choose between "this or that" photo for Instagram posts and for this book. Thank you for graciously accepting the role of "Instagram husband," practicing patience as you waited for the click of the camera before you could savor the dishes.

To my mom, dad, and brother for your unconditional love and for instilling in me a deep appreciation of nature and the beauty it brings to our lives. I am forever indebted to you for the love and beautiful memories.

To my dear friends and family, although I cannot individually list each one of you, please know that this book is a reflection of our collective stories. If any of the anecdotes or recipes within these pages resonate with you, it is because we have shared those moments together. I hope you recognize your significant contribution, knowing that you hold a special place. Without you, the wonderful memories that have served as the foundation for this project wouldn't exist.

To my online community and Instagram followers, your support, expressed through likes, comments, and messages, has been an incredible source of motivation and inspiration throughout the years. It's with you that I am always most eager to share my work first. Seeing your versions of the creations, tagged to my account, feels like receiving an excited message from a best friend who has just baked a cake, always bringing a smile to my face. I deeply value the sense of community we've created and the connections we continue to foster.

To my new readers, I really appreciate your curiosity and your open-mindedness in choosing this book. Thank you for giving me the opportunity to share my stories with you.

Whether you're a friend, family member, part of the publishing team, or a new reader, thank you for being part of this journey with me.

I look forward to seeing your take on the creations from this book. Please tag me on Instagram @celineyrs with your work, and let's continue to share in this journey together.

© Prestel Verlag, Munich · London · New York, 2024
A member of Penguin Random House
Verlagsgruppe GmbH
Neumarkter Strasse 28 · 81673 Munich

© Text and photographs: Celine Rousseau, 2024

Library of Congress Control Number is available;
a CIP catalogue record for this book is available from
the British Library.

The publisher expressly reserves the right to exploit the
copyrighted content of this work for the purposes of text
and data mining in accordance with Section 44b of the
German Copyright Act (UrhG), based on the European
Digital Single Market Directive. Any unauthorized use is an
infringement of copyright and is hereby prohibited.

Editorial direction: Claudia Stäuble
Project management: Veronika Brandt
Copyediting: Eve Hill-Agnus
Design and layout: Studio Mahr
Production management: Luisa Klose
Separations: Reproline Mediateam
Printing and binding: Mohn Media
Paper: Amber Graphic

Penguin Random House Verlagsgruppe FSC® N001967

Printed in Germany

ISBN 978-3-7913-8967-7

www.prestel.com